Every Child, Every Day

Every Child, Every Day

Achieving Zero Dropouts through Performance-Based Education

Michael K. Raible

ROWMAN & LITTLEFIELD
Lanham • Boulder • New York • London

Published by Rowman & Littlefield
A wholly owned subsidiary of The Rowman & Littlefield Publishing Group, Inc.
4501 Forbes Boulevard, Suite 200, Lanham, Maryland 20706
www.rowman.com

Unit A, Whitacre Mews, 26-34 Stannary Street, London SE11 4AB

Copyright © 2016 by Michael K. Raible

All rights reserved. No part of this book may be reproduced in any form or by any electronic or mechanical means, including information storage and retrieval systems, without written permission from the publisher, except by a reviewer who may quote passages in a review.

British Library Cataloguing in Publication Information Available

Library of Congress Cataloging-in-Publication Data Is Available

ISBN 978-1-4758-2114-7 (cloth : alk. paper)
ISBN 978-1-4758-2115-4 (pbk : alk. paper)
ISBN 978-1-4758-2117-8 (electronic)

∞ ™ The paper used in this publication meets the minimum requirements of American National Standard for Information Sciences Permanence of Paper for Printed Library Materials, ANSI/NISO Z39.48-1992.

Printed in the United States of America

Contents

Foreword		vii
	Roger Cook, the Taylor County Schools' superintendent	
Preface		ix
1	The Six Spokes of the Wheel	1
2	Accelerated Learning	9
3	Continuous Assessment	21
4	Virtual School and Early College	31
5	e-library	41
6	Early Release Fridays for Professional Development	51
7	Ubiquitous Technology	59
8	Career Pathways	71
9	S.T.A.R.S.	81
10	Student Ambassadors	93
11	Response to Intervention	101
12	Innovative Staffing	109
13	Continuous Validation	117
14	Collaboration	123
The Beginning		133
About the Author		137

Foreword

Roger Cook,
the Taylor County Schools' superintendent

I am honored and humbled that Mike Raible has asked me to write a foreword for his book on performance-based education, and specifically the methods used in Taylor County, Kentucky, where I am superintendent. My life's work has been education, but I am certainly not known for being much of a writer. I suspect that many people would never believe I would be part of a book like this. Here's why.

I was raised in poverty. I was the sixth child in a family of ten. Our family lived in a housing project in Campbellsville, Kentucky, and we had all of the classic characteristics of a dysfunctional family. My father was an alcoholic, who was fond of berating and beating his wife and children. My mother gave him many chances to become a better daddy and husband, but it just never happened. My mother divorced him, and remarried him. Then divorced and remarried him again. Finally, when I was ten, she kicked him out of the house for good.

My mother was a devout Christian and did her best to give her children the guidance we needed for success. We spent many hours in church on Sundays. That was the custom of my mother's True Holiness church. As you might imagine, it was very difficult for a ten-year old boy with a short attention span to sit for hours with my brothers and sisters on a hard bench. When not in church, my mother worked long hours in the Fruit of the Loom factory in town to make enough money to support us. She worked there until the day she died.

Six of my eight siblings dropped out of school. My brothers and I were always fighting, and it was not unusual for me to get into fights at school too. Then I began playing football. I could actually tackle someone on the field and be praised for it! But my trouble in school continued, and soon I was in front of the principal for fighting again. This time it was serious enough that I would be expelled. Luckily for me, my football coach intervened. If I kept my grades up and stayed on the football team, I would not be expelled. I stayed in school, continued playing football, and eventually graduated. Given my family situation and my short attention span, there were still many that doubted my ability to succeed, despite my high school diploma.

So how is this connected to a book on performance-based education? It is my district and my leadership team that this book is written about. Regardless of the obstacles I had to overcome as a child, I realized that I could be successful—education was the key to that success. If I had not stayed in school and graduated, I would not have found my life's work.

While this book will give you many of the details of what we have accomplished in Taylor County Schools, let me give you a few examples of how my experiences are connected to what we have done.

Many students in our schools have all of the disadvantages that I had growing up. We created a group of students called "Cook's Kids" to give them something extra in their lives. These students not only need more help with lessons at school, but also need something in their lives every once in a while—a special outing or a party. Everyone in the school system knows that these kids are special. Life has taught me that high risk does not translate to low expectations.

I don't believe that anyone should be allowed to fail, drop out, or be held back because of their age. The Taylor County Board of Education has supported me by adopting a policy of zero dropouts and a regulation that requires students to stay in school until the age of eighteen (local option permitted by the Kentucky legislature). We could not have accomplished what we have done without the enthusiastic support of the board.

Because I had a "short attention span" (now called ADHD), and got bored in school when I learned something and then had to wait until everyone in the class learned it, I have never understood why every student couldn't be challenged every day. Grouping by chronological age only serves to slow a student down. Our accelerated learning program allows students that have mastered content to move on and learn more. Even many of our elementary students are taking accelerated courses. Once they learn and then are given the opportunity to learn more, the momentum begins building. Many of our high school students graduate with two years' worth of college credits.

Football made school fun for me. I believe all education also needs to be fun. Our academic pep rally, which occurs just before state testing, is our way of celebrating every student's performance and randomly rewarding it. But we also reward our staff. Sometimes it's just a turkey at Thanksgiving, but as often as possible it is districtwide recognition and monetary rewards. We have a day near the Christmas holidays in which we reward every teacher, giving out the Roger Awards on that day too, recognizing the special efforts of nine teachers.

It is our responsibility to put each and every child in an environment in which he or she can be successful. I hope you will enjoy reading about some of the things we do to accomplish this.

Preface

> *Imagine . . . a school where students have no schedule or no teacher assigned to them.Imagine the freedom to learn in the way you learn best, with the teacher of your choice or none at all. Imagine not even being in a grade level. Imagine being allowed to take all the credits you want twenty-four hours a day seven days a week. Imagine graduation from high school as a sophomore in college. Imagine learning at your pace.* —2015 NSBA conference brochure for Roger Cook's presentation

The national statistics are awful. For every 100 low-income students that enter high school, only 65 will get a high school diploma, 53 will enroll in college, and 11 will actually complete a college degree.[1] And the statistics for students living below the poverty line are far worse. This is one of many reasons why Roger Cook and the Taylor County Schools is of particular interest. Any district with a 61 percent poverty rate and over 40 percent of students attending college and zero, yes zero, dropouts deserves to be examined.

Reforms of the educational systems in the United States and all over the world are coming from a wide variety of sources—philanthropists and businesses, federal and state governments, administrators and teachers, both large and small school districts. More nimble school districts have the best chance of creating a revised model of educational delivery that will produce successful students. Roger Cook and Taylor County Schools have proven that for the last six years.

From all outward appearances Taylor County School District is a typical 2,800 student school district located in Campbellsville, Kentucky. The district has an elementary school, a middle school and a high school. Their web site contains news of local interest and the slogan "Every Child, Every Day" used by many school districts in the United States.

Go to the first quick link connection on the site, About Our District. Performance-based education is explained this way, "Teachers do not teach grades, they teach students." And in the next paragraph their zero dropouts policy is explained. What makes Taylor County Schools unusual is that these are the facts, not the goals.

For the past seven years Roger Cook and his team have created a graduation plan for each and every student who has wanted to drop out. For the past six years this district and this superintendent have had a remarkable record—zero dropouts. This is a record that comes as a result of inspired leadership, unique delivery methods, and also from hard work.

If you were to select a superintendent most likely to succeed from a stack of resumes, Roger Cook would probably not be your choice. One of eight siblings born and raised in poverty, he was one of only two that have not gone to jail at one time or another. On the verge of being expelled for fighting with another student over a girl in school, he was rescued by the school's football coach. As long as he stayed on the football team, he could stay in school. Of course, he quickly realized that football was fun because people actually expected him to be rough on the other team. He actually received praise for it! Keeping up his grades (so that he could play football), kept him off the streets, out of jail, and allowed him to ultimately graduate.

After high school graduation, he started taking courses at Campbellsville University, but these were the Vietnam years and he had a low draft number. So in 1972 he was drafted. He spent two years in the Army and came back to finish his degree on the GI Bill. In 1977 while still working on his degree he got a job as a substitute teacher and assistant football coach at Campbellsville High School. After completing his bachelor's degree in social studies and psychology at Campbellsville University in 1979, he began pursuing a master's degree in psychology and counseling at Western Kentucky and still working at Campbellsville High, acquiring a passion for teaching along the way. He completed his education at Western in 1983 with rank one certification as administrator/superintendent.

His coaching career took him from Campbellsville High (1-A) to Breckinridge High (2-A) from 1981 to 1983. In 1983 he became the head football coach at East Hardin High (3-A). and then in 1988 he was named head football coach at North Hardin High (4-A), the largest high school in Kentucky at the time. He coached for three years at Hardin until stepping down to become the athletic director and assistant principal.

His most successful teams were at East Hardin. He built a good defensive team. His 1985 team is in the Kentucky High School Athletic Association record books as one of the teams that allowed the fewest total yards per season (1,425 in 11 games) and allowed the fewest rushing total rushing yards per season (748 in 11 games.) His teams earned two district championships and one regional championship during these years.

During the years of teaching and coaching, he began to see what worked and what didn't work both in the classroom and on the football field. He had his own ideas about what needed to be done. In 1995 he became the principal of Russell County High School in Russell Springs, Kentucky. He began to experiment with his innovative theories of education. But he was prevented from implementing his most creative programs. So in 2005 he became the superintendent in Russell County.

In 2006 he conducted a presentation with six other team members from the district on faculty, community, and student motivational programs that raise student achievement and promote community support. This was the beginning of his work on performance-based education. By 2008 when he presented to the National School Boards Association (NSBA) annual conference in Orlando, Florida, his topic was performance-based/competency-based education implementation strategies—his theories were now fully formed. In his final two years as Russell County's superintendent, the district had zero dropouts.

Then in 2009 he was asked to come back home to Taylor County and become their superintendent of schools. According to Board of Education chairman, Tony Davis, "We were a good little school system with dreams of becoming better." Roger Cook has made them realize their dreams. In a few short years he has turned Taylor County Schools into an organization of national reputation, a system with results any district would envy. TCS is an innovation machine in which not just a few executive staff or just a few early adopters, but the entire staff and the whole student body are leaning in for results.

Charles Higdon, assistant superintendent and former high school principal said that he could name over 100 innovative suggestions that he personally brought to Mr. Cook's desk over the past six years, and he couldn't think of a single one that received a negative response. Each and every one was an "Okay, let's try that and see how it works."

Of course, not every good idea works. And TCS leadership is quick to admit that. But Roger Cook gives every good idea a fair trial, and that's far better than in most organizations. He believes that you must lead from the front. It is his job to communicate the vision. He is an impatient, yet supportive leader. He wants to give every student the best environment in which to learn. But he wants it now, so that no student falls through the cracks.

For many that means accelerated learning, a system in which a student is not constrained by their age. For "Cook's Kids," a group of twenty-five high-risk, high-poverty students "like I was growing up," it means special attention to their needs. For all students it means a personalized education plan.

He has presented his ideas and results to the 2011, 2013 and 2015 annual NSBA conferences. He makes an important distinction between his ideas and many of the others. "This is not theoretical education reform. These are practical applications and verifiable results."

In 2015 the Kentucky Department of Education awarded Roger Cook the Dr. Johnny Grissom Award for exhibiting leadership, commitment, and service to promote high student achievement through instructional equity and in closing the achievement gap for all children. In 2014 the NSBA named Roger Cook one of the "20 to Watch" superintendents in the country. Also in 2014 the Center for Digital Education recognized Mr.

Cook for innovative uses of technology and education advancement. He was one of thirty honorees in the United States.

The changes Roger Cook has orchestrated and the results he has produced can be dismissed as too expensive, too difficult, or simply not applicable to your specific situation for whatever excuse you want to use. Performance-based education and the methodologies described are not for everyone. The point is Roger Cook has turned Taylor County Schools into an organization that not only gets every student a diploma, but gives them the tools for success in life. And isn't that what education is supposed to do?

NOTE

1. Nachazel, Thomas, and Allison Dziuba. *The Condition of Education 2014*. Washington: U. S. Department of Education, 2014.

ONE
The Six Spokes of the Wheel

There is a wall-sized square banner in the Taylor County School Board meeting room. It illustrates the six program delivery methods available to students. Like six spokes of a wheel, they fan out in all directions. Traditional, Project-Based, Peer Led, Self-Paced, Virtual, and Cardinal Academy. This is your first clue that education in Taylor County is not the norm. "We figure out how each and every child performs best and that's where we put them." —Roger Cook

THEORY

In their book, *Lessons Without Limit: How Free-choice Learning is Transforming Education,* John Howard Falk and Lynn Diane Jierking write in praise of learning that is self-directed. It is the essence of a lifelong learner. And what makes it so attractive to each individual is the freedom of choice, "choice over what, why, where, when, and how we will learn."[1] This is what the six spokes are about. Taylor County Schools are responding to parent and student interests by offering various choices.

Daniel Pink writes about the three motivators for improving complex tasks—autonomy, mastery and purpose. Although motivation is a critical element of education, very few school systems have been able to change their pedagogy in a meaningful way to truly address Mr. Pink's findings. In fact, everything from pay-for-performance to various schemes for student reward and punishment operate in direct opposition to Pink's findings. He says, "Too many organizations—not just companies, but governments and nonprofits as well—still operate from assumptions about human potential and individual performance that are outdated, unexamined, and rooted more in folklore than in science."[2] There is no evidence that additional extrinsic reward motivates improvement in complex tasks like teaching and learning. He cites the research of Harry Harlow[3] and Edward Deci[4] as proof.

AUTONOMY

The basis of autonomy is the luxury of choice within four elements: task, time, technique and team. Choice of task (i.e. the manner in which the academic program is delivered to the student) relates directly to autonomy. Traditionally, educators pick a delivery method that they feel has been successful for them or one that piques their interest.

The element of choice in this case not only creates autonomy of task, but also creates buy-in. If a teacher has selected a preferred method of delivery as a pathway for his or her students to be successful, it reinforces their commitment to ensure student success.

Therefore, when a student chooses a program delivery as their preferred method of learning, it creates their buy-in. The student selects a preferred method of learning for each class on their schedule and with that, they bring a certain amount of commitment to ensure that they made the correct choice.

The choice of time is provided either through 24/7 access to instructional lessons or by the student's selection of a specific time and place to receive instruction. In each case there is an opportunity for the students to self-pace, acquiring the knowledge at their own pace and then demonstrating their acquisition of those skills and knowledge through measures of academic performance.

While students are not given the opportunity to rearrange their grade assignment, they are given the opportunity to select their team. The autonomy of team is addressed by the students being able to select their instructors, their classroom, and the instructional delivery method that is the best fit for them.

PRACTICE

Roger Cook begins his presentations by explaining that in order to change outcomes, it is necessary to put every student in an environment in which they can learn best. While he originally designed his methods of performance-based education to respond to the needs of those students who were not successful in a traditional environment, it turned out that students at the other end of the academic spectrum also benefited from the variety of educational delivery methods he created.

TCS begins scheduling classes for the next school year after the winter holidays. The first step is filling out an on-line survey. This gives the district ample time to make sure they have accommodated each student's needs. Each student has a personalized instruction plan that includes information about their goals and career aspirations as well as their assessment results. A student will select not only a group of courses of study for the next school year, but also the instructor and the delivery method for each course.

Roger Cook doesn't like standing still. So like much in this district, the six spokes are also a work in progress. Eventually each course description will be written around one of the spokes and each student will build an annual schedule based upon the best instructional methods for them. But even as that occurs, it is anticipated that the best of blended learning will occur within each spoke. Clearly, a teacher in a traditional class in which each student has an electronic device will not stand before the students and lecture for the entire class. So while the courses will be put into one of the six boxes, the actual instructional delivery may use any or all of the tools available.

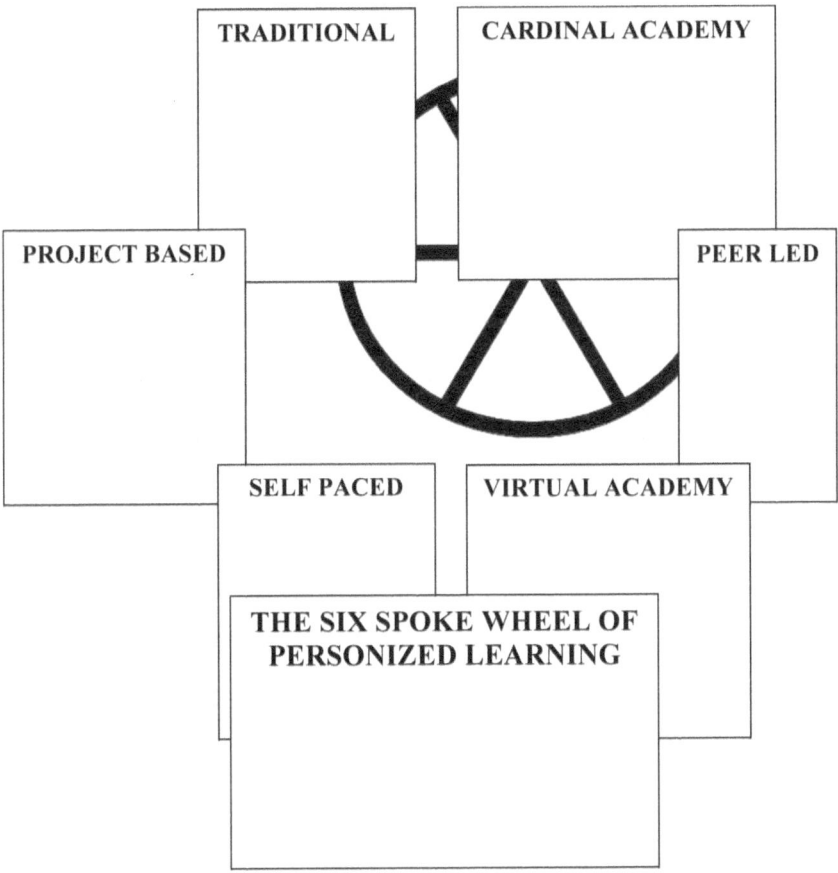

Figure 1.1.

Cardinal Academy

More than 200 students a year apply to attend the Cardinal Academy. Less than half are accepted, although Cook hopes to increase that number in the future. The Academy is a rigorous independent study curriculum offered to high school students and soon to be offered to middle school students as well. The room used by the students of the academy looks more like a student lounge than a traditional classroom. There are tables and chairs, but also abundant soft seating. There is substantial technology. What is missing is a teacher.

The six academic coaches of the Cardinal Academy each have an advisory of ten to twelve students. These students determine their course load and schedule. The structure resembles independent studies in college. At any given time the student's advisor knows where their student plans to be, but the Academy students are not supervised. It is up to them to meet the previously agreed upon academic standards.

Assistant Superintendent Charles Higdon Jr. is the senior staff member responsible for the Academy. He says the application process is as strenuous as that of a first-year teacher at Taylor County. Students who want to be admitted fill out the same written application as a teacher applicant. They must demonstrate ability through their assessment results (distinguished or proficient). They must acquire recommendations from their teachers regarding their maturity, and they must be selected through a difficult interview regimen.

Cardinal Academy students get to pick their schedule and their teachers. They can choose to study a course on-line or in person. They can take traditional or self-paced classes. They can take university classes on-line or at the local campus. It is their choice, assuming there is a correlation with their personalized instruction plan.

Peer-Led Classes

Casey Young teaches American History and an introductory psychology/sociology course at Taylor County High School. In his introductory course, which is an elective, he uses the peer-led model.

He began this as an experiment because he realized that he was not covering his course content at the pace and depth he had planned. He decided to divide the remaining content by the chapters in the textbook and asked pairs of students to prepare and teach that content in a way they felt most comfortable learning it. Both teacher and student learned from this experience. Mr. Young learned that students could be creative about explaining psychology and sociology and, of course, the students gained deeper knowledge of the subject by teaching it.

If there were a student assistant assigned to his class, Mr. Young would likely use that student to lead instruction as well. As the number of students in the S.T.A.R.S. program (see Step Nine) increases, the number of peer-led courses will expand as well.

Teachers in Taylor County enjoy the freedom of participating in a very innovative environment. That means they have the ability to design a different instructional delivery system that is best for each course they teach. So while Casey Young's elective course is peer-led, his American History course is project-based. There are successes and failures with each new technique that is tried. Each is discussed with fellow educators during the Friday meetings within the professional learning communities and replicated, modified or discarded based upon the results.

Virtual Academy

If there is one tool in the box that has given Roger Cook the ability to create an educational environment where dropping out is not an option, it is the Virtual Academy. It gives students access to on-line courses twenty-four hours a day, seven days a week for credit. It gives TCS the scheduling flexibility to adapt to the students' issues that often cause them to think that dropping out of school is the only alternative. Some of the turnaround stories from the Virtual Academy are remarkable.

A student and her parent came to the superintendent's office for a dropout request. The student was pregnant and saw no way that she could continue her education. Mr. Cook suggested that with the Virtual Academy she could take classes on-line and return to school once she had the baby. She explained that she had no computer and no Internet access from home. Cook arranged for her to receive both. The student worked with the Virtual Academy to take her classes while she was out of school on maternity leave. She now has a high school degree and is on the dean's list at the local university.

A defiant tenth grader with a history of drug use was a student that most educators would classify as a likely candidate to drop out. He was rescued by a TCS team that included an at-risk coordinator, his counselors, the virtual teachers, and the school administrators. The team meets with him frequently and reviews his progress. This student is now working diligently on his on-line classes and is actually on track for early graduation.

A high school junior who hated her classes and was habitually truant last year has now completed three on-line classes and is making excellent grades in her other classes, all of which she attends regularly.

An eleventh grade student who moved from home to home, was unmotivated and was unsuccessful with classes last year, making it almost impossible to graduate with her classmates. Since working in the Virtual Academy, her attitude has changed, her level of effort has changed, and she has completed enough courses at this point that it looks as though she will graduate with her classmates.

Self-Paced Classes

Because of his experience in school where he felt he was forced to review material he knew already, Roger Cook wanted to create an environment where kids were not held back when they mastered the material. He saw the Sal Khan episode of *60 Minutes* and wanted to bring "flipped" classrooms to Taylor County. A typical flipped classroom is one in which the lesson is delivered via technology. The student learns the content on-line, usually at home, and then works on the assignment (the homework) in class where the teacher is able to assist. So, the lesson is at home and the homework is in class, therefore a "flipped" classroom.

Cook and the team realized that the technology could also be used to accelerate learning and allow the acquisition of content at the student's own pace. So, instead of a typical flipped classroom in which all students move through the content at the same pace, they wanted to allow students that understood the work to move through the material at their own pace.

However, as the team had their first meeting and began looking at the pro's and con's to the approach, they decided that they needed something more than a flipped classroom model. Jessica McCubbin and Sarah Hayes, two of the team members, developed their own self-paced model. They called it "self-paced flipping" at first, then dropped the "flipping" part because it really had its own identity.

Of course, this requires a significant effort by the classroom teacher at the initial stages of the program. Teachers must prepare at least twenty-five video lessons, fifteen to twenty minutes in length, at the beginning of the school year for each course. A total of ninety content videos are needed for the entire school year. Each teacher monitors the student progress because their production of content videos must out-pace the students' consumption. Once the videos are made, the work is somewhat easier, since then the preparation involves editing the videos for the next year and not recreating them.

Those teachers that have converted their classes say they will not go back to traditional methodology. The idea that a teacher can spend class time working with the students that are struggling, and allowing those that are not struggling to move up to the next lesson, is very seductive. It puts the teacher precisely in the place where they can do the most good and puts each and every student in an educational environment where they are challenged.

Traditional Methodology

There are some teachers and students at Taylor County Schools that prefer the traditional educational delivery. And for those, there is the traditional spoke of the TCS wheel of educational practice. In the scheme of things these teachers and students are not shunned, nor are they seen as unequal partners. This is one spoke of the wheel of educational delivery and it is a critical methodology, just like the rest. But they are less popular with teachers. Cook observes, "I used to have to pay teachers extra to participate in self-paced classes. Now I feel like I have to pay extra to get them to teach in traditional classes."

The TCS traditional spoke looks more like blended learning than a standard lecture course. Just as in other classes, technology is used to supplement and deliver content. Just as in other classes, students are divided into small groups for class assignments or discussion. One of the only differences is the pace of instruction. There is little opportunity for a student to move ahead of the instructional pace of the rest of the class with traditional delivery.

Traditional teaching methods have certainly produced many successful individuals. There are simply some students who are unable to understand content that is delivered this way. The other spokes of the wheel exist for those students. Differentiation between subjects is also possible at TCS. Students are not tracked into traditional or self-paced and required to take all of their courses from one delivery method. For example, it is possible to select traditional delivery for language arts and self-paced for math. Just as with the other delivery methods, each student at TCS receives a personalized education schedule tailored to their needs.

Project-Based

The sixth spoke of the wheel is a project-based delivery system. Some students find it helpful to understand the practical application of the skills they are learning. For those students a project-based delivery method makes sense. Taylor County Schools has created nine student enterprises that provide career-based training in everything from banking to automotive service.

There is an Apple certified repair service at the middle and high schools. There is a Kroger store at the high school. At the Fancy That gift shop students learn inventory and retailing skills selling everything from screen-printed and embroidered school spirit items to candles and gift baskets and items from the woodworking shop. The Cardinal Corral is a catering business that provides meals for events in the school community. An auction site called tBay, sells items on-line. T-Signs makes signs for all sorts of programs. And the FFA Greenhouse gives students the chance to seed and cultivate flowers, herbs and vegetables.

Red Bird Rinse does auto detailing during the school day. A student-run bank provides small loans and savings accounts for teachers and students. There is an aviation program for those students interested in flying. Studio Red is a program that designs and produces marketing material for the schools and the community.

A wide range of career-based training is also offered through the 14 career majors in the Career Technical Education program.

This is all about offering programs that pique students' interest and get them thinking seriously about a career. Mr. Cook says, "If I had a student interested in underwater basket weaving, I'd find a way to offer it."

The career pathways are dealt with in detail in a later chapter. By their junior year each student is asked to indicate a career preference. Those career categories include:

- Education, both early childhood and K–12
- Finance
- Engineering and Technology
- Visual Art and Graphic Design
- Culinary Art and Food Service
- Marketing and Retail Services
- Instrumental and Vocal Music
- Agriculture
- Aviation

Student work inside each of the categories varies depending upon the career they intend to pursue. For example, a student interested in sports marketing might be involved in marketing for the athletic teams, whereas a student interested in retail marketing could be involved in co-operative employment at one of the local retail stores.

The purpose of this spoke of the wheel is twofold. First, TCS wants to provide practical application of the content that the students are learning in the academic courses. And second, Taylor County wants to be sure that students acquire the "soft skills" that make all the difference in success after graduation.

NOTES

1. Falk, John Howard, and Lynn Diane Jierking. *Lessons without Limit: How Free-choice Learning is Transforming Education.* Walnut Creek: AltaMira Press, 2002.
2. Pink, Daniel H. *Drive.* New York: Riverhead Books, 2009.
3. Harlow, Harry F. "Motivation as a Factor in the Acquisition of New Responses." In *Current Theory and Research in Motivation*, by Judson S., Harry F. Harlow, Leo J. Postman, Vincent Nowlis, Theodore M. Newcomb and O. Hobart Brown Mowrer, 43. Lincoln: University of Nebraska Press, 1953.
4. Deci, Edward L. "Intrinsic Motivation, Extrinsic Reinforcement, and Inequity." *Journal of Personality and Social Psychology*, 1972: 119–20.

TWO
Accelerated Learning

"If they can prove that they know the material, why should they be made to suffer through a whole series of lessons they already know? That's educational abuse." —Roger Cook

THEORY

Age-Related Grouping

Malcolm Gladwell has written extensively about age-related groupings. In his book, *Outliers, The Story of Success*, he discusses the phenomenon that most A-level hockey players in Canada were born in the first three months of the calendar year. The youth leagues in Canada are organized by age. A nine-year-old whose birthday is January 1st plays with nine year olds that are up to twelve months younger than him. The best young players are selected at nine and ten years old from youth leagues grouped by age. Of course, the ones singled out for further coaching and higher level play are the biggest and best coordinated players—and generally they are the oldest in the age group.

"The way Canadians select hockey players is a beautiful example of what sociologist, Robert Merton, famously called a 'self-fulfilling prophesy'—a situation where 'a false definition, in the beginning . . . evokes a new behavior in which the original false conception comes true.' Canadians start with the false definition of who the best nine- and ten-year-old hockey players are. They are just picking the oldest every year. But the way they treat those 'all-stars' ends up making the original false judgment look correct."[1]

But this issue doesn't apply just to hockey and to Canada. In the United States where the cutoff date for non-school youth baseball leagues is the end of July, the "best" players are born in August. Gladwell again cites statistics. Among Americans playing major league baseball in 2005 (*Outliers* was published in 2008), 505 were born in August and 313 in July. Far more than other months.

He goes on to explain that these biases are even prevalent in education, where parents of children born near the end of the year hold their children back a year. Gladwell refers to research that indicates a significant difference in ability of up to 12 percentile points at ends of the age group. He says, "It means that if you take two intellectually equivalent fourth graders with birthdays at the opposite end of the cutoff date, the older student could score in the eightieth percentile and the younger one could score in the sixty-eighth percentile. That's the difference between qualifying for a gifted program or not."[2]

Although the dictionary defines intelligence as the ability of acquiring and applying knowledge and skills, it is not that simple. As Gladwell is quick to remind us, we often misunderstand intelligence. Robert Sternberg theorized that there are actually three types of intelligence: analytical intelligence, the ability to problem solve when there is one correct answer; synthetic intelligence, the application of existing knowledge to solve problems with several right answers; and practical intelligence, the ability to adapt to conditions in everyday life.[3] When we test a fourth grader to determine giftedness, we are testing analytical intelligence.

Our species are pattern seekers. Our ancient ancestors that survived in the savannah were the ones who could tell the difference between the wind and a predator moving in the tall grass. As we mature, we gain the ability to separate useful information from useless information. The brain of a child is acquiring this information at an incredible speed. "A typical American seventh grader knows the meaning of 10–15 words today that she did not know yesterday."[4] And all indications are that knowledge acquisition is even faster when we are younger. Then it should be no surprise, that older students test on grade level or above more often than the younger students. But how do we structure the delivery of educational programming to respond to this phenomenon? Clearly annually grouping by age may not be ideal.

So why do we continue to move our students through the educational assembly line grouped by age (grade level), and measure a school's status by the percentage of students on grade level? We even celebrate our ability to get students through high school "on time" by reporting a four-year graduation cohort as the graduation rate. But is that really cause for celebration?

Platooning or grouping students by age (i.e. grade) was a component of the Prussian system of compulsory education much admired for its efficiency by American education reformers in the nineteenth century. The hierarchical Prussian model grouped students by age and not ability. Education reformer Horace Mann promoted the Prussian model, with its depersonalized learning and strict hierarchy of power, because it was the cheapest and easiest way to teach literacy on a large scale. This system was perpetuated throughout the early twentieth century by social efficiency theorists who sought to industrialize the educational process. Grouping by age was included in the State of Michigan Constitution of 1835, which introduced a continuum of primary schools, secondary schools, and the University of Michigan itself, administered by the state and supported with tax-based funding. Mann convinced the governor of Massachusetts to adopt a similar mandatory education system in 1852. The first graded school in the United States opened in 1848 as the Quincy Grammar School in Boston, Massachusetts.

So the Prussian education structure and hierarchical philosophy were transplanted and sustained in America for efficiency, although grouping by age actually diminishes the results for the younger students in the grade level. Many other attempts at education reform have also concentrated on structural efficiency. In the 60s and 70s we believed that schools without walls would improve education. The structure alone, although more efficient to build, also did not change outcomes. More recently we came to believe that small schools would yield better academic results. But again, we found without a change in program delivery, the results didn't improve. In each case structure did not change outcomes.

So why do we have to group by age? Primarily because we have constructed such an elaborate system of accountability built on the concept of a student being on grade level. Prior to the "No Child Left Behind" federal legislation and its corresponding accountability standards, several states briefly flirted with the idea of multi-age education. Kentucky established multi-age primary programs in 1990, and in 1992 required that every primary program have the following: developmentally appropriate educational practices, multi-age and multi-ability classrooms, continuous progress, authentic assessment, qualitative reporting methods, professional teamwork, and positive parent involvement. Although regional service centers with primary education consultants were established in 1992, the funding was discontinued in 2003. And although multi-age primary programs have shown some promise, the Kentucky demographic survey describes a reduction of multi-age classes since 2001.

The State of Michigan started a grant program in 1994 for "the establishment of non-graded continuous progress programs for students in multi-age classrooms," but the grant funding ended in 1999. Incompatibility with grade-level content and the annual testing cycle were some of the reasons given.

When public education was first made available and compulsory to the public, its stated purpose was training of the workforce and the sorting of that workforce into two groups: labor and management. Those who excelled were on track to be the future managers, a small group.

Those who did not were the future laborers, a much larger group. There was some crude logic to this sorting despite its randomness because you could still earn a living wage whether you were labor or management. There were far more jobs for laborers than for managers, and so the numbers roughly balanced.

Not so today. This random sort between management and labor now means college-bound versus career-bound. Trouble is, the careers in which someone can earn a living wage without a certification or a college degree are scarce. In fact, some analysts speculate that the numbers needed are actually reversed. So the timed sort no longer yields the results it was created to generate. This brings the whole idea of knowledge acquisition and the speed of that acquisition into question.

Maturity or Intelligence

Is someone that learns more slowly actually less intelligent or will that student ultimately be less knowledgeable? It depends.

If you look at Gladwell's hypothetical fourth graders, who are intellectually equal, but one scores significantly better than the other at the time of annual testing. Does it really matter? The real question is should it really matter? Not if both were given similar training and advantage. We would not be able to tell the difference between the two as adults. But without the opportunity to learn at their own pace, the older (supposedly smarter) student will be given educational advantages that the younger student will not be given . . . and all because that student is younger, not "slower."[5]

In fact because the symptoms of immaturity and attention deficit hyperactivity disorder (ADHD) are similar, many of our younger students are not only classified as less able, but in many cases diagnosed with a disorder and prescribed a regimen of medication. In an article in the November 20, 2012, issue of *The New York Times*, Anahad O'Conner reported on a study which found that the lower the grade, the greater the disparity. For children in the fourth grade, the researchers found that those in the youngest third of their class had an 80 to 90 percent increased risk of scoring in the lowest decile on standardized tests. The study also found that the youngest third of the students were 50 percent more likely to be prescribed stimulants or any other medications for ADHD.[6]

Guidance

Whether we annually group students by age or by ability, we are still grouping students. Individualized performance-based education provides an opportunity for students to acquire knowledge at their own pace. But this must be a guided journey, not just wandering in the wilderness.

There was once an amusement park built up river from Cincinnati, Ohio. In the 1950's one of the rides for young children was a racetrack complete with gas-powered cars. The cars were fitted with angle irons on the undercarriage and the extensive track had a rail down the center. So while the roadway had guardrails on either side (just like the go-cart track for the big kids) and the cars traveled pretty fast if you pushed the gas pedal all the way to the floor, your mistakes in steering to one side or the other were limited by the rail down the center and the steel angles under the car. If the car stalled while on the track, the pit crew would come out and get it running again. Many kids drove slowly at first. But as confidence grew, they went faster and faster until some went at top speed through most of the track. The excitement of being able to race on your own at a very young age was intoxicating. You can imagine, it was a very popular ride.

Individualized performance learning is very much like that. You are learning in a safe place—between the rails. You are on the track. You cannot get off. But you can control your journey. You can go slowly at first, if that feels less risky to you, and faster as you gain confidence. You can take the corners on the inside or on the outside. It is up to you.

Pace

The second part of the graded vs non-graded theory has to do with pacing. Teachers tend to target their instruction to the abilities of the middle third of the students in the class. Differentiation of instruction (i.e. the delivery of the lesson to each student according to their ability) is difficult at best and more frustrating as the span of student abilities and the number of students assigned to a classroom have increased. The result is that the students who struggle are lost, and the student who instantly understands is bored. Pacing guides and standard-course-of-study manuals tend to approach the acquisition of knowledge as a timed test. If a student grouped by age with his or her peers acquires and remembers a sufficient amount of knowledge for his or her grade (proficiency), he or she is said to be "at grade level." In most cases this is made official through the results of an annual high-stakes test, often administered by the state department of education for whichever state in which the student resides.

In 1993 the former Harvard Graduate School of Education dean, Dr. Patricia Graham, testified before the National Commission on Time and Learning. She stressed that while time had been the constant and learning the variable for more than a century, she said that "in the future we must hold learning high and constant and make time the flexible variable."[7] The logic behind performance-based education is that all children don't learn to walk or talk at the same age, so too measuring a student's ability annually on a single day is not an appropriate measure of his or her ability. Grouping by age, rather than by accomplishment, makes no more sense than identifying the walkers and the talkers at the age of twelve months as the children who will be college-bound. Dr. Graham's testimony goes directly to the issue of pacing. Whether because they are not attuned to the initial knowledge delivery the first time around, or because they are less mature than some of their classmates, some students simply need more time to acquire the knowledge.

Performance-based education means that even if you are not an experienced runner, that with a substantial head start you can race anyone and win. This is the view of time that we must adopt for our students. If you are teaching a diverse class of thirty students, but of the same age and the time allotted in the pacing guide has expired, then you must move on in order to cover the rest of the curriculum by the end of the year.

It becomes a matter of re-teaching until that student finally "gets it" and slowing the learning for the rest of the class, or moving on and hoping somehow that eventually that student will catch up. Neither is a good option, but it is a decision that teachers all over the United States face every day.

Personalizing education and self-pacing allows students to progress at their own pace. Those that need spend a little longer on some content can do so, receiving help, but not holding the rest of the class back. And those that understand the lesson immediately can move on to other challenges.

PRACTICE

In the age of "No Child Left Behind" accountability, creating ungraded public schools is almost impossible. What Taylor County Schools does is use age grouping and the grade structure as a threshold from which to launch an accelerated education program with proficiency and mastery as the expectation. Instead of every child can learn, TCS says no child will be allowed to fail. In theory that sounds like a license for wholesale social promotion. In practice, it means that each and every teacher does everything possible to make each child successful.

While it would seem the best odds for improving outcomes would be to concentrate on those students who are testing just below grade level, a no child allowed to fail policy creates the expectation for every student to be at grade level or above. On a four point scale the question is not how many 2's can get to 3, but how can everyone get 3's and 4's.

Age is not a criteria for placement in Taylor County Schools. If a student demonstrates proficiency, they can move up to the next level. Nearly one-fourth of elementary students are in an accelerated program. Some spend all day in upper level classes, others take a single class and then return to their grade level for the rest of the day.

Student data is reviewed every week at the professional development sessions held every Friday from 1:00 pm until 3:00 pm. (This is an early release day every week.) If in the opinion of the educational team, the child is ready to be moved up, then they are moved. Most of the complaints about this program come from the parents of students who have not been allowed to accelerate. This becomes a powerful incentive for the student to improve and the parent to support the improvement. Students must be in the 90th percentile or higher on the MAP assessment and AIMS web and be proficient or distinguished on the state assessment or equivalent classroom performance (for those who move in from out-of-state or are in a grade which has not taken the state assessment). Parents must agree to allow their child to take accelerated classes, if the classes are to be offered on another campus (e.g. a fifth grader taking algebra at the middle school).

Attitude

In an educational environment that celebrates its "proficient and progressing" rating, it would be easy for the superintendent to exert an enormous amount of downward pressure on the staff to perform with greater and greater effectiveness. And although Roger Cook believes that inspiration comes from the top down, there is less emphasis on the numbers and more emphasis on the individual child. Of course, there is pressure on the teachers to make the students successful, but it is about the student's acquisition of knowledge and skills to make them successful and not about test scores.

High stakes testing has spawned a few incidents of teachers cheating at school districts with the same goals as TCS. Roger Cook certainly wants the good results too, but his focus is how learning will improve the lives of his students. To this end, he has created a system that is flexible enough to effectively accommodate the learning diversity of his students. And while high test scores are one indication that the learning is occurring, it is this personal connection between staff and students that makes the difference.

One student this year experienced issues at home that forced him to work more hours at his job to take care of his family. Unfortunately, that put him in a position of getting further and further behind in his work at the high school and even further away from his desire for a career in auto mechanics. The staff at the high school worked out a program of virtual offerings for his required credits, classes in auto mechanics at the Greene County Area Technical Center (in the adjacent county), and a schedule that put him on track to graduate and still allowed him to work the additional hours he needed to support his family.

While a multitude of districts claim student success as their mission or as one of their goals, TCS tries to listen to their students and actively demonstrate they genuinely care about students' success both inside and outside of the classroom. The middle school music classroom is lined with guitars hanging on the wall. They teach guitar because it is an instrument that is fun for the students to learn and offers them an opportunity to demonstrate their expertise outside of the school environment. There is an avionics class at the high school because students expressed an interest in learning to fly. A few have now earned their pilot's licenses. There is a Kroger store at the high school, not only because students in the CTE classes can learn about merchandising, but also because teachers can use the store instead of stopping to pick up convenience items on their way home. There is a student operated bank at the high school. Forgot your lunch money? It is easy to get a loan from the bank. It is this attention to detail that sets them apart.

Time

TCS understands that some students need more time on a lesson than others. More and more teachers in the district are making their daily lessons available 24/7 on the Internet and on a thumb drive for those that do not have an Internet connection at home. These are not canned lessons pulled from an unknown teacher somewhere in the ether, but a lesson prepared and presented by the child's teacher because they have found that the personal connection to a student's teacher makes a difference. Each teacher films their lessons with the help of two staff members well-versed in the delivery of effective electronic lessons. These two technical advisors (both teachers themselves) are invaluable resources to those unfamiliar with the details of putting lessons on line.

Self-pacing also occurs in many of the classrooms. Quarterly formatives (Measures of Academic Progress) as well as teacher-created assessments are used to diagnose a child's daily acquisition of skills and knowledge. In the self-paced classrooms each child records their progress often on a poster on the wall and in a notebook that resides in the classroom. Assessment data is reviewed by each academic team on early release Fridays each week.

Just as there are teachers and students that opt for the traditional educational delivery, so too there are some students that stay within their class group for the entire school day. There is no censure for this. It is simply viewed as the student's preference.

Remediation

In a mostly 1:1 student to electronic device environment, there is a substantial amount of remedial assistance available. One teacher had a student home with the flu. He was able to follow the lesson online, and the technology permitted the teacher to see his work and give him assistance where necessary. She was pleased that although the student could not come to class because of illness, he was able to keep up.

There are other tools and techniques to assist struggling students available as well. There is the tutoring and peer coaching described in another chapter. In situations where the teacher feels the student is falling too far behind, they can use Response to Intervention. This technique allows the child to recover without having to wait until the next testing cycle. It is an opportunity to triage the problem and schedule remediation before the issue is compounded.

There are about twenty students that the superintendent calls "Cook's Kids." These are students that are at high risk for academic failure. Roger Cook is particularly interested in these children "because they are dealing with the issues that I had to deal with growing up." Additional academic resources are given to these students, including making sure they are assigned the best teachers.

There are 120 high school students in the Cardinal Academy. This is self-directed and self-paced education. Although these students make the faculty advisor aware of their schedule, it is up to them to accomplish the work. Some Cardinal Academy students attend classes, others use the virtual academy, still others attend college courses at the local university.

Many TCS students graduate high school with enough college credits to enter a university as a mid-term sophomore. The current tuition at Campbellsville University is 350 dollars per credit hour. TCS students can attend for 60 dollars per credit hour. It is estimated that last year's graduating class saved over 268,000 dollars in tuition. Of course, they have saved far more if they plan to attend a private or out-of-state institution.

Cook wants to get graduates to return and teach. With almost two years of college completed, some Taylor County High School graduates will be able to compete for teaching positions with an additional two years of college.

Logistics

Administrators begin scheduling classes for students in January. This allows plenty of time for students to decide what they might be interested in taking the following year. Once classes begin in the fall, teachers begin reviewing outcome data every week. If it is the consensus of the team that the student should be moved up, the student is re-assigned.

Every Friday is an early release day. This is professional development time. Data on every student is reviewed and possible changes in assignment are discussed as well as other student performance-related issues.

TCS students from pre-school to twelfth grade ride the bus together. There are two adults on each bus, the driver and a bus monitor. Shuttle buses move students between campuses during every period of the seven-period day. Five minutes are allowed for passage between classes. It is accepted that some students will occasionally be late to class. It is not a cause for alarm.

Many, but not all, teachers do self-pacing with their students. It is generally accepted that once converted, teachers never go back. This is a common interview statement from teachers. "I love teaching this way. I'll never go back. If I have to leave here, I don't know where I would go because I don't want to teach the old way anymore."

One of the waivers TCS has been given as an Innovation District in Kentucky is for how they account for students. Like most states, Kentucky contributes to the operation of the school district on the basis of average daily attendance. As you might imagine with virtual classes, the independent study of Cardinal Academy and the students taking early college classes accounting for ADA is a challenge. And yet, because attendance is so important to performance, a great deal of effort is exerted to identify absentees and contact their homes to verify their whereabouts.

Cook says that he finds teachers no longer notice the ages of the students in their classes. If a fifth grader shows up in a high school class, it is so much the better. Perhaps it may serve as an incentive for the older students to try harder, so they are not embarrassed by the ability of the younger student!

Flexibility

Multi-age and accelerated educational groupings require flexibility. The teachers have learned to teach whoever comes in the door. Those that are used to empty hallways except during class changes get used to students in the halls even during class time. Some programs have flexible attendance like Cardinal Academy and the Virtual Academy, but it is also a result of the flexibility of instructional groupings. During one visit there were groups of four and five students clustered in the halls at the middle schools. They weren't socializing; the discussions were instructional. They were all sitting on the floor working on lessons on their iPads. Different students learn in different ways. One of the film crews from a local news program showed a student laying with his back on the floor and his feet on the wall working on his iPad. Roger Cook's comment was, "As long as he is learning . . ."

Small communities still have their share of troubles. And a multi-age grouping that allows no child to fail has to be flexible to deal with it. One student had a history of drug addiction, a difficult, almost non-existent home life, and trouble with the law. This is the kind of student that would typically fall through the cracks. But with a zero drop out and no child fails policy in the district, the staff continued to reach out to him. The at-risk coordinator, the school counselor, and the virtual school teachers continued to work with him. He has turned out to be a really hard worker and is on track to graduate a year early. He is currently only one credit short of that goal.

Another student, age eighteen, was emancipated, and was on his own. He has a baby to support and was working at Subway. He got a job offer at Amazon for the full-time day shift, but he had to report almost immediately. He was put online in virtual academy and needed two classes to graduate. He completed those classes staying after school every day and finished the day before he was scheduled to start at Amazon.

Another high school student needed multiple credits to graduate. He was frequently absent. He often skipped classes, and had a long history of drug addiction. His mother owned a trucking company and told him she didn't care if he finished school or not. She would give him a job as a truck driver regardless. He was in the court system for truancy and did not show any signs of progress. He tried online classes at home unsuccessfully. Then he asked if he could attend TCS Virtual Academy at the high school and work on completing his credits. In December, he began working diligently at the academy. He completed his required classes prior to the end of the school year, and will graduate this year. Without program flexibility, he would not have graduated.

These are not isolated cases. Every student has a story about how Taylor County Schools adapted the program to fit their needs, or responsibilities, or career goals. Success has less to do with a policy that does not allow a student to drop out or a rule that does not allow a child to fail. The difference is the attitude and flexibility of the staff. Not only are the expectations high, but also the authority and permission to do what it takes to accomplish those expectations is freely given.

NOTES

1. Gladwell, M. (2008). *Outliers, The Story of Success*. New York: Little, Brown and Company.
2. Gladwell, M. (2008). *Ibid*.
3. Sternberg, R. J. (1985). *Beyone IQ: A Triarchic Theory of Intelligence*. Cambridge: Cambridge University Press.
4. Dumais, T. K. (1997). "A Solution to Plato's Problem: The Latent Semantic Analysis Theory of Acquisition, Induction and Representation of Knowledge." *Americam Psychological Review*, 211–40.
5. Gladwell, M. (2008).
6. O'Conner, A. (2012, November 20). "Younger Students More Likely to Get A.D.H.D Drugs." *The New York Times*.
7. Doyle, D. P. (2004, April 26). "Grouping Kids by Age Should Have Vanished with the Little Red Schoolhouse." *The Los Angeles Times*.

THREE
Continuous Assessment

This is not about passing or failing, it's about knowing. No matter where you are headed, it is necessary to measure your progress so that you know where you are. Since mastery is our goal, we regularly measure our students' progress and share the results. —Susan Kilby, Taylor County Schools' assistant superintendent

THEORY

Testing in all forms has almost become a pejorative in education. Included in the *Harvard Business Review*'s list of breakthrough ideas for 2007 was David Weinberg's piece on the *Folly of Accountabalism*. In it he says, "Because accountability suggests that there is a right and a wrong answer to every question, it flourishes where we can measure results exactly. It spread to schools—where it is eating our young—as a result of our recent irrational exuberance about testing, which forces education to become something that can be measured precisely."[1]

However, measurement of a student's progress is necessary in education. Susan Kilby, Taylor County's Assistant Superintendent responsible for testing says, "Without testing, neither the teacher nor the student can evaluate the quality of the teaching and learning that has occurred."[2]

Terminology

Robert Glaser first categorized tests as either norm-referenced or criterion-referenced.[3] The items (questions) in a criterion-referenced, or standards-based, test are written to determine whether the test taker possesses certain knowledge that is established in advance. (e.g. State end-of-course or end-of-grade tests that measure knowledge of a standard curriculum.) Norm-referenced tests are created to sort test takers into a relative ranking according to the number of questions answered correctly. IQ tests are norm-referenced tests. There is no way to pass or fail a norm-referenced test, you just do better or worse than the others who take the test.

There is also a difference between a test that is given by one teacher in one subject to a group of students and a test that is given by all the teachers of a specific course to all of the students enrolled in that course. The latter test is called a common or standardized assessment. The advantage of a common assessment is that it can be a criterion-referenced test, telling each teacher what each of their students has learned. Because every student has taken a similar test, it can also be used to compare outcomes from other teachers' students. As a result of an increasingly hostile working environment, common assessments have become "high stakes" tests used to measure not only student progress but also teacher effectiveness.

As if the vocabulary wasn't complex enough, criterion-referenced tests are periodically updated or improved to adjust for changes in subject matter or curriculum as well as improving the clarity of questions. Typically when this is done, test scores for common assessments go down. Because common assessments are also used to sort students based upon their scores, these periodic adjustments are referred to as "re-norming."

The tests used to gage student progress during the school year are called formative assessments. Those that are used to test what a student learned during a course of study are called summative assessments. It is rare that a school or district will make the results of formatives public. They are specifically used internally and shared only with students, teachers, parents and school administration. These are diagnostic in nature and not the "high stakes" tests that cause high anxiety for students and teachers.

Summatives, on the other hand, are used for comparisons between schools and districts. They are accountability tests.[4] Many states are also beginning to use them for teacher evaluations, basing a teacher's eligibility for performance pay on the summatives.

The results of formatives are usually available in a matter of days, if not immediately. However, the results from summatives can take months to be published.

Standardization

Without an agreed upon common measurement there can be no meaningful comparisons. A GPA of ninety from one school could be a "B," while from another it could be an "A." Clearly, the same is true of test scores. Without a common definition of what is to be studied and tested there is no way to compare the outcomes from one district to another.

State departments of education have been aware of this issue and have mandated for quite some time that students take common assessments in "core subjects." The results of these assessments are then used to compare and contrast school districts within the state. But there is no national test. The closest thing to a national test is the National Assessment of Educational Progress (NAEP). It is a test given to randomly selected students in grades four, eight and twelve in mathematics, reading, science and writing. Other subjects such as the arts, civics, economics, geography, and U.S. history are assessed periodically.

The 2001 No Child Left Behind Act required that states which receive Title I funding from the federal government must participate in state NAEP assessments in reading and mathematics at grades four and eight every two years. State participation in other subjects assessed by state NAEP (science and writing) remains voluntary. In 2011, twenty-one urban districts also participated in the Trial Urban Districts Assessment (TUDA), but as of this writing there is still no common assessment across every state and every school district, and therefore, no accurate way to compare outcomes across schools in different states.[5]

By 2014 a total of forty-three states and the District of Columbia had adopted the Common Core Standards which set unified expectations for what students in kindergarten through twelfth grade should know and be able to do in each grade in math and language arts. This has also created a testing controversy. Since it is the purpose of the Common Core that students prove proficiency of an aspect of a specific subject, it is no longer sufficient for the students to be tested solely through multiple choice exams. Just as when a common assessment is revised and the scores are initially lower, so too when the Common Core tests debuted the scores were lower.

In all but a few isolated cases, the standardized tests are used in a limited number of subjects. In general the "tested subjects" are about one third of the total courses offered by any school or district. Although the outcry about testing has been loud and long, most educators realize that in order to be able to accurately compare the quality of education, testing will have to occur across a broader spectrum of courses than just math and language arts. The trouble is the existing regime of testing has already created a firestorm.

Frequency

Like any other skill, test taking improves with practice. A skillful test taker is less anxious and uses the allotted time carefully. But even a good test taker that has no or limited knowledge of the subject will not be able to produce a good outcome.

Author and executive coach, Marshall Goldsmith, believes in frequent measurement. He and Jim Moore, former Chief Learning Officer of Sun Microsystems and a close friend of Goldsmith's, check in with each other every day and review a pre-determined set of questions about the important issues in their lives. Jim asks Marshall the same twenty-four questions. Marshall asks Jim the same seventeen questions. Marshall and Jim maintain a spreadsheet of each other's questions and they record the daily answers. They exchange the spreadsheets on a weekly basis.

Goldsmith says, "This process works because it forces each to confront how they actually live their values . . . every day. You find you either believe that something matters or you don't. If you really believe it, you can 'put it on the list' and do it! If you really don't want to do it, you can face reality and quit kidding yourselves."[6] Frequent measurement is critical to knowing where you are and how you are doing. This is true in school as well as life.

PRACTICE

Assessments at Taylor County are diagnostic. Their purpose is to measure student progress and to make adjustments to instruction. "Think of assessment, then, as information for improving. This idea takes a while to get used to if you teach, test, and move on. The research could not be clearer, though: Increasing formative assessment is the key to improvement on tests of all kinds, including traditional ones."[7]

Formative assessment at TCS is continuous, occurring several times during every class. Whether traditional or self-paced, each class has roughly the same flow. First, the class studies subject content outside of the classroom, either through homework (traditional) or by reviewing an instructional video (self-paced). Next is an initial exercise called a bell ringer. This is followed by a content lesson and assignment. And finally, there is an exit assignment.

Bell Ringer

The first assessment is called a bell ringer. Bell ringers are used in both traditional and self-paced classes. This is usually an exercise on a personal electronic device. The exercise is correlated with the common core pacing for the school year. The content students should have covered the previous day is the bell ringer topic/question the following day. This helps the teacher gage progress in the content they should have learned and gives the teacher a chance to identify students who are still struggling or who are not where they need to be with the content.

All students in the class participate in the fifteen minute bell ringer. It is an opportunity for the teacher to review previous lessons (for those students that have moved ahead) and to develop skills (for others that are struggling with a specific lesson).

Students use EduCreations, an interactive whiteboard application, to write their answers to the bell ringer. Once all students have finished, everyone holds their iPad up to be quickly scanned/checked by the teacher. The teacher or tutor identifies those still struggling and they gather a small group to help those students while others move on with new content.

If you are in a traditional classroom, the bell ringer is a way for the teacher to make sure you understood what was taught and that the instruction was appropriate. In the traditional classroom the bell ringer is effectively the daily quiz. Regardless of the method of lesson delivery, students are presented with an unfamiliar problem and are asked to apply the knowledge they have acquired. In all cases, the bell ringer is not simply multiple choice or true/false or delivery of some memorized material.

Since the bell ringer is tied to the pacing guide, it establishes the floor, the minimum content knowledge required. Those that are able move on and those that have accelerated spiral back for a review during the bell ringer. While the common core pacing is the floor for every student, there is no ceiling for self-paced students. They can move through the curriculum as fast as they want, as long as they can demonstrate they have mastered the material. No student is permitted to fail. Everyone masters the material. Many students move beyond the minimum.

Self-Assessments

After the bell ringer, the classes focus on a content lesson. Those that are self-paced work by themselves or in groups on their tablets. Those in traditional classrooms work on content with the teacher.

Many teachers take this time to have the students perform a self-assessment. By color-coding their name as they work through the assignment, students identify themselves as red, yellow, or green. Those that are colored red are in need of additional help. They are having difficulty understanding the content. Those that are colored yellow are unsure about the content and believe they require more work either individually or in groups. Those students that are green understand the content and are either moving on or tutoring other greens or yellows. There is no stigma attached to needing help on the day's content. Self-assessment is a way for students to take responsibility for their own success and academic improvement.

Presentation of Content

Some teachers prefer to deliver the course content in the traditional manner. And some students prefer to receive it that way. Other teachers prefer to deliver content in a self-paced classroom. This requires a significant amount of initial work, since the teacher's fifteen- to twenty-minute content lessons must be videotaped and posted to the web. Although, the teachers that have done that believe that ultimately this creates a more effective classroom because they can personally concentrate during class time on the individual struggling students.

Most teachers use some form of visual progress chart to keep track of their classes. These charts, with stickers indicating completed work, are often posted prominently in the classrooms. This is another way for each student to monitor their progress and a quick way for the teacher to see if an individual student is not keeping up with the rest of the class and needs additional assistance.

Since performance-based education is about students demonstrating mastery, all teachers concentrate on a questioning methodology that avoids multiple choice or true/false answers. Questions in class and in the exercises encourage the application of acquired knowledge to new problems and higher-order thinking, not memorization.

When Roger Cook arrived at Taylor County Schools, he sent an e-mail to staff about what he wanted to accomplish and the tools he wanted to use. In that e-mail he asked for volunteers to begin working within the new system of assessments. The math teachers were the first to volunteer.[8] Math instruction has matured in the use of technology-adapted formative assessments. The middle school math instructors use the Carnegie Learning[9] and elementary school math teachers use Singapore Math.[10]

Common Assessments

Assistant Superintendent Susan Kilby, an eighteen-year TCS testing veteran, would like to have common assessments more frequently, but students in Taylor County Schools already take a formative common assessment created by the district every nine weeks. This is for diagnostics and analysis. How well do the students understand? Can the program delivery be improved? Do the videos deliver the content well?

District-prepared common assessments involve a significant amount of staff time. The goal is to offer diagnostic common assessments more frequently, but the amount of staff time it takes to prepare them in-house means progress toward that goal will be slow.

There are other common assessment tools available to Taylor County teachers. The Continuous Instructional Improvement Technology System (CIITS) is a multi-phase, multi-year technology project of the Kentucky

Department of Education containing a lesson-planning tool and scheduler to help teachers with standards-based instruction in their classrooms. Teachers can also share instructional resources that they design through CIITS.[11]

Teachers are able to build their formative assessments using a test item resource of more than 11,000 items. Tests are then administered online or with a student response system and teachers are able to see student progress immediately. Instructional experiences can then be created to address the learning gaps highlighted through the on-line assessments.

"Aggregate and student-level demographic, program and performance information in CIITS allows educators to easily see how students are progressing toward Kentucky's goal of every student being proficient and prepared for success and graduating college/career-ready. Interim assessment data as well as PLAN, EXPLORE, ACT data is available through CIITS."[12]

End-of-course and end-of-year summative data is also uploaded to the site. And a "Dynamic Key Performance Indicators" section allows teachers to choose from pre-formatted reports or build their own custom reports for data analysis.

The district uses Measures of Academic Progress a computer adaptive formative assessment product from Northwest Evaluation Association[13] three times a school year. These assessments are used as diagnostics as well as preparation for the summatives at the end of the school year. The results are also one of the data points used when discussing whether or not a student should be accelerated.

Google forms are used by several teachers in the district to administer quizzes and tests to students digitally. Forms provide immediate feedback to both the teacher and student. The Google script, Flubaroo, grades the assessments that have been submitted and also organizes students' responses into a spreadsheet.[14]

Analysis

Susan Kilby says it is not sufficient for the educators to possess all of the data from testing. It is important that the data be shared with the students and given to the students' families, so that everyone knows where they are and what is expected. The data will give the educators the tools to plan the instructional path for the students and will give the students the knowledge of where they are on that path. But before they can share, teachers and administrators must understand the data.

Taylor County Schools hosts a three-day off-site data retreat prior to school start. One teacher from each grade level is invited to participate. During this retreat the teachers are given the tools of data analysis. They are taught both how to look ahead and how to look at history through data analysis. These grade-level representatives understand that it is up to them to teach the others in their professional learning communities about the process of data use and analysis. In this way they are given ownership.

Frequency

Test taking at TCS is approached as a skill, just like driving a car or using a computer. In order to master that skill, a student must practice it so that test taking becomes second nature, a common occurrence. The high frequency of assessments tends to remove anxiety from the exercise because they become routine and "not a big deal."[15] And since the goal is mastery, not memory, the assessments are not multiple choice or true/false tests, but measurements of higher order thinking and problem solving.

This is one third grade teacher's reading warm-up about comparison and contrast:

> Mona and her twin, Lisa, went to the library on a rainy afternoon. Mona went straight to the magazines. She liked reading about her favorite actors. Lisa looked at the poetry books. Lisa picked up a couple of books and went to look for her sister. They sat down at a table together and read while the rain fell outside. How are the sisters alike? How are they different?[16]

Using the Data

No student fails in Taylor County Schools. There are many reasons. Tests of any kind (even the standardized state tests) are not viewed as pass/fail events. Yes, some are more important than others, but none is a game changer. If the purpose is to teach and learn, then tests are simply a way to gather information along a student's journey to mastery. Jessica McCubbin and Sarah Hayes, Technology Integration Specialists at TCS, study a student's exit exams as carefully as they study a student's common assessments in the fall. These results are a window into what is left to be done. They use these results to identify additional remedial work for the journey toward mastery.

These are not quarterly discussions among teachers after report cards are issued or parent/teacher conference material. Analysis of data occurs every week at every level through various professional learning communities. School principals report weekly to central office administrators about future plans for professional development and past results of data analysis across grade level or content level professional learning communities.

NOTES

1. Weinberger, David. "The HBR List: Breakthrough Ideas for 2007." *Harvard Business Review*, 2007.
2. Kilby, Susan, interview by Michael Raible. Assistant Superintendent (March 3, 2015).
3. Glaser, Robert. "Instructional technology and the measurement of learning outcomes." *American Psychology*, 1963: 519–22.
4. Wolf, P. J. "Academic Improvement through Regular Assessment." *Peabody Journal of Education*, 2007: 690–702.
5. "National Assessment of Educational Progress." National Center for Educational Statistics. April 21, 2015. http://nces.ed.gov/nationsreportcard/ (accessed May 15, 2015).
6. Goldsmith, Marshall, Marilyn McLeod, and Andrew Thorn. "Peer Coaching Overview." Marshall Goldsmith Library. 2007. www.marshallgoldsmithlibrary.com/docs/articles/Peer-Coaching-Overview.pdf (accessed March 17, 2015).
7. Wiggins, Grant. "Healthier Testing Made Easy: The Idea of Authentic Assessment." *Edutopia*. April 3, 2006. http://www.edutopia.org/authentic-assessment-grant-wiggins (accessed June 15, 2015).
8. Kilby, Susan, interview by Michael Raible. Assistant Superintendent (March 3, 2015).
9. Carnegie Learning. 2015. https://www.carnegielearning.com/learning-solutions/implementation-models/ (accessed March 16, 2015).
10. Singapore Math. 2015. http://www.singaporemath.com/ (accessed March 16, 2015).
11. McCowan, Joseph. "CIITS Overview." Kentucky Department of Education. January 6, 2015. http://education.ky.gov/curriculum/ciits/pages/default.aspx (accessed March 16, 2015).
12. McCowan, Joseph. "CIITS Overview." *Ibid*.
13. Measures of Academic Progress (MAP). 2015. https://www.nwea.org/assessments/map/ (accessed March 16, 2015).
14. Hayes, Sarah, and Jessica McCubbin, interview by Michael Raible. Technology Integration Specialists at Taylor County Schools (March 3, 2015).
15. Kilby, Susan, interview by Michael Raible. Assistant Superintendent (March 3, 2015).
16. Sanders, Jade. "Sample 3rd Grade Reading Unit Checklist (Compare and Contrast)." Taylor County Schools. December 9, 2013. www.taylor.kyschools.us/userfiles/1297/Jade%20S_%203rd%20Grade%20Reading-Unit%204-Week%201%20Checklist%5B2%5D.pdf (accessed May 15, 2015).

FOUR
Virtual School and Early College

The room is vast. It feels like it could hold a hundred students. There are over 60 desktop computers lining the perimeter. It is lunch time and yet several students are working with headphones on, intently studying their screens. There are also two clusters of students quietly discussing a common topic. The students are focused and the discussions are animated. This is the TCS Virtual Academy, what Roger Cook famously called his "illegal charter school."

THEORY

Virtual schooling is a program of academic courses taught primarily through the use of technology. It is a learning platform in which students move at their own pace through a broad variety of courses and earn credits toward graduation. There are cyber schools in which a student is offered a full course of study, and there are virtual programs that offer students an opportunity to take one or more online offerings for acceleration or remediation of required credits. Some students use virtual schools for elective courses.

The Early College High School program provides a rigorous academic opportunity for high school students to acquire college credits. Courses are either dual-certified for high school and college credit or college courses for credit. Courses are offered on the high school campus or on a college campus depending upon the location of the venues.

The Basics of Virtual Education

Virtual classes were first used as a way to provide access to a wider variety of classes for students in small and/or rural secondary schools. The classes were either offered as a live broadcast (called synchronous) or as a self-paced formatted lesson (called asynchronous).

Virtual course and school providers include for-profit vendors, school districts, consortiums or districts or states, charter schools, and a variety of state education authorities. One of the largest of these is the Florida Virtual School (FLVS) begun in 1997. Its 2013–2104 enrollment was 197,924 students. FLVS offers over 120 courses to high school students on line and over 12,000 hours of professional development for educators. Students and teachers from all over the world use the resources of FLVS.

School districts have also created virtual schools. Some have created stand-alone courses of study for their secondary students, and others have utilized available resources from the Internet. Whether vendor-designed, state-sponsored or district-created, there does not appear to be a common recipe for virtual education. The only thing that they all have in common is the delivery of educational program through electronic means.

In their 2012 report entitled, *Searching for the Reality of Virtual Schools,* The Center for Public Education concluded that, "digital content in public education is therefore not a matter of debate; it is inevitable. But school leaders and education policymakers do need to consider how to manage the influx of online learning opportunities in order to make sure students get their full benefit and not end up lost in cyberspace."[1]

Proponents of virtual schools point to the self-pacing and the ability to individualize the instruction based upon the student's progress as benefits. The advent of the Internet has been accompanied by a profusion of virtual post-secondary schools. Many of the college classes are offered as synchronous classes, since that allows the instructor to communicate with the class as a group. Many other virtual offerings, including those for high school credits, are offered as asynchronous classes, that is a student can proceed at their own pace without having to be online at a specific time for class discussions or lectures.

The availability and high quality of online classes has also increased the number of students that are schooled at home. Home school teachers that lack subject expertise can rely on virtual classes to deliver specific content with which they are unfamiliar.

However, Taylor County has found that taking courses at home without benefit of a specific time or access to a subject matter expert requires self-discipline and maturity that many students do not possess. The challenge of staying focused at home on academic studies with all of the distractions of the home environment is one reason that virtual school students without guidance do not appear to perform as well as regular education students on standardized tests as students in more typical school environments.

Regular monitoring and coaching are critical to the success of a virtual education program. For this reason the successful student working on their own without an adult monitoring their progress is rare. The number of completers for massive open online courses is only seven to nine percent.[2] Most successful virtual programs are used as a supplement to traditional teaching. (This is called blended learning.) Or the virtual learning occurs as part of a program in which progress is monitored frequently. (This is the Virtual Academy.)

The Benefits of Virtual Education

In their collection of essays titled, *Virtual Schools, Planning for Success*, Berge and Clark list four benefits to virtual schooling: expanding educational access, providing high-quality learning opportunities, improving student outcomes and skills, and allowing for educational choice.[3]

Expanded access takes many forms. It can mean access to higher level math courses for those students in rural or small schools. It can mean access to courses in the Mandarin language for a student in a large urban school. It can give a student a second chance to pass a required course in language arts. It could mean that a student unable to schedule a course that was only offered once during the school day would still be able to take that course at a time that was more convenient.

Providing high quality learning opportunities is another advantage. Delivery via technology allows for revisions and edits. The lessons can be revised and rewritten as much as needed before they are uploaded. And once completed, the perfected lesson can then be reused. Of course, professionally filmed and edited lessons are also available. High quality lessons also mean lessons that provide current information. While Language Arts and Math tend to change slowly if at all, lessons in science and social studies could change year to year. Being able to deliver lessons that contain current material invariable increases the quality of the lesson.

Virtual lessons, if used appropriately, can improve student outcomes and skills. The ability to replay a particular lesson or portion of a lesson may improve student outcomes. Access to supplemental material often included in virtual lessons also increases cognition. Virtual remedial lessons give students the opportunity to revisit their work. The re-teaching often comes built into the lesson as the student answers the quizzes.

The issue of educational choice may mean that a student can select which course to work on at any given time. This provides the student some autonomy in regard to their work and allows them some freedom. The student's progress monitor can provide guidance so that choice still produces successful outcomes

The Disadvantages of Virtual Education

A student that lacks the personal discipline to continue to work on the virtual content on their own time, may have difficulty completing virtual courses. As previously stated the completion rates for MOOCs are not exemplary.

Commercially available virtual lessons are not easily personalized. For that reason Technology Integration Specialists Sarah Hayes and Jessica McCubbin find that lessons prepared and videotaped by the student's teacher are far more effective than lessons available through the Internet. They attribute this to the personal connection between the students and their teacher. They actually coach the teachers to add comments into the videotaped lesson like "I know some of you are saying what does this have to do with math . . . that is what you're saying isn't it, Jimmy?" to get and keep the student's attention.

Verification of knowledge acquisition is problematic, particularly if the goal is not simple memorization of facts but rather the ability to apply the knowledge acquired.

The Basics of Early College

The early college delivery model changes to fit the available circumstances. If offered on a high school campus, the courses are often taught by a college instructor and are college credit or dual credit (high school and college) courses. If students attend a college campus, the courses are generally college level courses for college credit. If the courses are offered virtually, they are usually for college credit. Those school districts that are fortunate enough to have a post-secondary institution in close proximity to the district have a little more flexibility when it comes to venue and course offerings. Many colleges are happy to work with school districts to register students for early college courses in the hope of filling classrooms during off-peak hours (late morning and early afternoon. Other colleges and universities are glad to have access to high school students because they often continue their college careers at the same institution.

The Advantages of Early College

College experience is almost a necessity in today's society to earn a living wage. Anthony Carnivale and his co-authors at the Georgetown Center On Unemployment and the Workforce have said in their 2011 report that even some college credit (but no degree) increases lifetime earnings by 18.6 percent. They found that the difference between a person with a two year degree and a high school graduate is an increase of 32.4 percent in lifetime earnings. Any level of additional education translates to an increase in wage-earning over a lifetime. "These numbers prove that higher education opens up the highest-paying jobs, but also that there is a range of pay within jobs and that more highly-educated people usually earn considerably more than their less-educated counterparts in the same occupation."[4]

Clearly, it is no surprise that early college programs have increased exponentially since their start in 2002. Even if the student does not take advantage of the head start toward a degree that college credits deliver, they will nonetheless see an advantage in exposure to a broader base of knowledge and ultimately a higher lifetime income.

Research from the Bill and Melinda Gates Foundation Early College Initiative indicates that 81 percent of students in an early college program enroll in college after high school.[5] And since enrollment immediately after high school is a good indicator of degree attainment,[6] it follows that the more students register for post-secondary education following high school graduation the more college graduates you will have.

One of the reasons that parents and students alike are drawn to Early College programs is the cost savings. In many cases college credit or dual credit courses are offered to high school students at a reduced rate. With the average college tuition and fees exceeding 30,000 dollars per year, the two years of college credit that can be accumulated by a diligent high school student adds up to substantial savings.

PRACTICE

The Taylor County Virtual School and the Early College Program work in tandem to provide students with choices. Those choices include credit recovery, advanced courses, career and technical training courses, foreign language courses and college courses.

The Lab

There are between 30 and 40 students scheduled to be working on the more than sixty desktop computers in the virtual academy at any of the seven periods during the day. The main lab is located in the current high school which when the new high school building is completed will become the middle school. Originally, the space was an open courtyard between two buildings on the high school campus, but Cook decided that it would make a good tech lab and set about on his own with a little bit of money and a metal building design to turn it into a technology showplace.

In most schools students get various forms of negative reinforcement so that they understand there are consequences to their actions. Superintendents in the State of Kentucky are required to attend courses related to their infractions. This lab cost Roger Cook to attend a six-hour class in ethics because instead of following KDE procedures for design, bidding and construction, he proceeded to work outside the department's guidelines (including using his personal construction equipment) in order to build the structure within his budget.

Three full-time staff members and a whole host of teachers "mind the store." About the only time there are few students in the lab is lunch time. The activity not only includes students working on and being coached through an incredible array of on line lessons, but also drop-in focus groups (clusters of five or six students with an accountability partner) using the labs programs and courses for remediation, planning, or anything else that will get them back on track.

Flexibility

The secret to the success of the virtual academy is flexibility. The staff believes they can design a unique program to meet the needs of every student that walks through the door. There are self-paced students that take almost all of their required classes by computer. There are students whose schedules were unable to accommodate all of their interests. There are students who have failed a class and want to stay on track to graduate with their peers. There are students who are unable to attend a full day of classes. And there are adult learners from the community who because of a life circumstance were never able to get a high school degree.

The virtual academy also works with organizations in the community. There is one company that will hire an employee that lacks a high school diploma as a part-time employee. If they agree to attend the virtual academy to get a diploma, they are given a full-time job upon graduation.

Access to academic material 24/7 is somewhat taken for granted at Taylor County. One of the waivers that TCS sought from the Kentucky Department of Education as a district of innovation (one of the first in the state) was the opportunity to use computerized lessons during snow days. They call them "cyber snow days." The lessons are prepared in advance, and when inclement weather is predicted, all students are asked to participate in the cyber lessons. The participation is about 98 percent. Those that do not have Internet access are given a removeable drive that contains the lessons.

Each student at the virtual academy is required to log on and work on their assignments on a regular basis. For those who have a scheduled period in the lab, that means every school day. This work is largely self-paced, although help is available if needed. If the majority of students happen to be taking social studies in third period, the staff arranges for a social studies teacher or two to be available for questions and assistance, likewise for math or language arts.

The virtual academy is a critical tool for getting to zero dropouts. This is a district with 60 percent economically disadvantaged students. One of the major reasons that students and parents give for wanting a student to drop out is the need for money. The virtual academy can provide the required scheduling flexibility for a student to work in the co-op (early release) program after fifth period. Or a program of study can be designed that allows a student to work more hours, if that is necessary for financial support.

Success Stories

There are many success stories from the virtual academy. Two students that became parents and got married felt they had no choice but to drop out of school to work and support the family. The staff of the academy designed a schedule of classes for them that allowed them to work and care for the infant as well as providing the flexibility for day care during the inevitable days that the baby was sick. Both students graduated and stayed in the community.

One young man transferred from another school system three courses short of graduation. He was truant and had behavioral issues and was told by his former district that it would probably be better for him if he just dropped out. But the courts did not agree. He was ordered back to school. He worked hard at the virtual academy and received a diploma finishing those last three courses that he needed.

Another student with two siblings that were seniors in high school was not on a path to graduation. Drugs, alcohol, and a dysfunctional family all got in the way. His dad was in jail and his mom didn't know where to find him most of the time. But then a program specifically designed for him in the virtual academy changed his attitude and he caught fire. He will graduate this year and pursue a career working with his hands. He likes making furniture. He also likes farming. Regardless of what he chooses, his teachers are confident that he will continue to be a credit to his community.

And then there are all of the students in the Early College program. The staff estimates they have saved the students and their parents a minimum of 286,000 dollars in college tuition. Many are able to graduate with a bachelor's degree in two years.

Rigor

The virtual academy is not summer school on a screen or technological social promotion. These classes are as rigorous as the face-to-face classes and in fact, are arranged to be in sync with the TCS curriculum map. Whatever instruction the students would get in class is exactly what is delivered to them on line. This is intentional. The unintended consequences of a relaxation of standards would be poor academic outcomes on standardized tests. Assistant Superintendent Charles Higdon reported that during the final year of the No Child Left Behind regimen, TCS was the only district in the state to comply with the requirements of the legislation and have zero dropouts.

Rigor is also clearly a part of the Early College program. Many courses of study are available on-line. The College Now program is offered in cooperation with Jefferson County Schools. Campbellsville University and Western Kentucky University offer on-line credit courses to TCS students. There are dual credit courses (high school and college credit) offered at the high school taught by staff certified at the post-secondary level. There is a full array of Advanced Placement courses and the requisite testing for college credit available to TCS students.

In some cases the advanced students need to take the ACT in their freshman or sophomore year in order to qualify to take the Early College courses. Again, an enhanced accelerated academic program has to offer students a full range of choices once they have completed the requisite courses for high school graduation. For Taylor County students it has become a reason to stay.

Although the Kentucky Department of Education offers an early high school graduation program to students that have completed the required credits, not many TCHS students apply. The vast majority of Taylor County students that enroll in college choose Campbellsville University, and the tuition is much less expensive for high school students than for high school graduates.

Some seniors remain even though the cost for them to attend a post-secondary institution is the same as other students. A handful of students have attended other Kentucky colleges and universities: Lindsey Wilson College in Columbia, Western Kentucky University in Bowling Green, and Eastern Kentucky University in Richmond. While they maintain a full course load at those institutions, these dual credit students (they receive high school and college credit) still do not want to miss the senior experience—dances, athletic events, graduation, etc.

The key to successful academic momentum is to never stop. There is no such thing as senior slump at TCS. The 24/7 access to rigorous academic programming provides students with the confidence, the initiative and the maturity to be successful in college and in life.

The virtual academy is one of Roger Cook's signature programs. In his testimony before the Kentucky legislature in 2013, he called it his "illegal charter school." It is a substantial weapon in dropout prevention. But it is not a one size fits all program. Jennifer Fitzpatrick Taylor County's director for their Virtual Academy says it's not about thinking outside the box. This program has no box. Its success is due to be creative and flexible in designing something for each individual student's needs. This is student-centered education at its finest.

NOTES

1. Barth, Patte, Jim Hall, and Rebecca St. Andrie. *Searching for the Reality of Virtual Schools*. Alexandria: The Center for Public Education, 2012.

2. "MOOC's on the Move: How Coursera is Disrputing the Traditional Classroom." *Knowledge@Wharton*. November 7, 2012. knowledge.wharton.upenn.edu/article/moocs-on-the-move-how-coursera-is-disrupting-the-traditional-classroom/ (accessed May 18, 2015).

3. Berge, Zane L., and Tom Clark. *Virtual Schools, Planning for Success*. New York: Teachers College Press, 2005.

4. Carnivale, Anthony P., Stephen J. Rose, and Ban Cheah. *The College Payoff*. Georgetown: The Georgetown Center on Unemployment and the Workforce, 2011.

5. Berger, Andrea, Lori Turk-Bicakci, Michael Garet, Joel Knudson, and Gur Hoshen. *Early College, Continued Success: Early College Intitiative Impact Study*. Washington: American Institues for Research, 2014.

6. Adelman, C. *The Toolbox Revisited: Paths to Degree Completion from High School through College*. Washington: U.S. Department of Education, 2006.

FIVE
e-library

"This is a simple issue of access. If our lessons are available 24/7, but the school library is only open on school days, then we have limited our students' access to knowledge. The e-library gives them a reliable source of information that is always accessible." —Roger Cook

THEORY

The American library movement began in 1876 with the founding of the American Library Association (ALA) by a group of librarians including Melvil Dewey, the founder of what is termed "library science." In the late nineteenth century a school library, if it existed at all, was a collection of single volumes of books accumulated by the teachers as additional reading material for the advanced students.

School Libraries

The first national standards for secondary school libraries were the result of the research conducted by the Committee on Library Organization and Equipment (CLOE), chaired by Charles C. Certain. They were adopted by and published by the National Education Association (NEA) in 1918 and adopted by the ALA in 1920. These standards attempted to describe and quantify the components of a good high school library.

The "Certain Standards," as they came to be called, addressed the need for high school libraries to become an extension of the school academic environment by setting goals, planning, and establishing quantified collections, seating, and equipment. The hiring of an appropriately trained librarian was also part of the standards.

The school library became a media center as a reflection of the change in the materials that the library was being required to store and catalog for easy reference. In the 2004 longitudinal study of school library media centers, the National Center for Educational Statistics reported that school media centers were multi-tasking. "The types of technology and equipment that many libraries had (and the percentage that had them) were Internet access (96 percent), personal computer (94 percent), VCR (91 percent), audio equipment (89 percent), telephone (88 percent), and automated book circulation system (74 percent)."[1]

It is also apparent from the report that the school media center in 2002 (when the survey was taken) was a physical place in the school building. The majority of the respondents (93 percent) indicated that the school media center configuration was centralized, described as in one area in one building. It is also interesting that 75 percent of the media centers responding had fewer than 16,000 volumes in their inventory.

The student survey that was the basis of the report had questions about student use. Students reported that they used the school library materials sometimes or often for research papers (54 percent), for school projects (53 percent), for Internet access (41 percent), and school assignments (41 percent).

The report also indicated that economically disadvantaged students used the library "sometimes or often for assignments" and in-school projects.[2] Students with high test scores were more likely than students with low or middle scores to use the library for assignments, in-school projects, and research papers.

Purpose

The school library or media center functions as the source for all information available. Traditionally, the school librarian or media specialist provides expert access to those resources and is the arbiter of the appropriate use of reference materials. Is an encyclopedia better than an article in a magazine? How reliable is a peer-reviewed article in a market-sponsored periodical? What kind of information can be used from newspapers? Is every newspaper a reliable and quotable source? Is it possible to use a work of fiction as a source?

For example, Thomas Piketty in his scholarly book on economics, *Capital in the 21st Century*, uses the references to wealth in well-known novels of the nineteenth and twentieth century to illustrate the changing assumptions, context, and concepts of wealth through the ages.[3] This is not a typical reference source, but one that works well in this particular work. Given the subject of the book, another economist might hesitate to use the references, but a skilled librarian would likely encourage or even suggest such a connection.

But in the age of unlimited access to digital reference materials, the dilemma for educators is how students are to be advised as to the appropriate reference materials. This is certainly a part of being a responsible digital citizen.

Outcomes Related to Access

A study from Illinois looked at schools that provided increased access to the school library through flexible scheduling, and it found that when compared to students in those schools with more restricted access fifth grade students performed 10 percent better in reading and 11 percent better in writing on the Illinois Standards Achievement Test (ISAT). On the American College Testing exam in Illinois high schools, there was a 5 percent difference between the outcomes of students in schools with increased access to school libraries and those students in schools with more restricted hours.[4]

A study in Michigan found that students and teachers in schools with the highest reading scores on the Michigan Educational Assessment Program (MEAP) were four times more likely to have access to a library collection on a flexible schedule than those in schools with the lowest scores.[5]

Cost

In their February 14, 2015 post to their Internet site, the *School Library Journal* reports the cost of school library books in 2014 to be between 6.56 to 8.28 dollars for each paperback and 19.47 to 26.44 dollars for each hardcover.[6] For a high quality school library, most state guides like North Carolina's call for the number of volumes per student average about twenty.[7] That means a school population of 2,500 students should have access to 50,000 volumes. If the collection is half paperback and half hardcover, the average cost of purchasing the inventory new in 2014 would have been 759,375 dollars.

To purchase a collection of 50,000 volumes of e-books in 2014 at an average cost of twenty dollars per digital book[8] would cost 1,000,000 dollars.

Since the two totals (759,375 and 1,000,000 dollars) were both a result of averaging and various other assumptions, they may not be an accurate dollar for dollar comparison, but the difference in order of magnitude is remarkable. The purchase of a digital library is clearly more expensive, and it also requires that each and every student has access through an electronic device (tablet, e-reader, netbook, laptop computer, desktop computer, or smart phone), and the cost of those devices is not included in the e-book total. Digital devices and student access are discussed in chapter 7.

Security

Bill Brown is the Executive Director of Education Technology Services for Greenville County Schools in Greenville, South Carolina, and an expert in cyber security. Greenville has nearly ninety schools. All of their schools have access to digital material, but four of them have completely eliminated their traditional hard copy libraries, relying exclusively on digital libraries. Brown believes that as digital libraries become more commonplace, they will become the targets of hackers because the books are loaded on all devices.

Although this pathway could be used to insert malware into the system, the malware would have to be fairly sophisticated to circumvent the device support of the e-books. He thinks most hacks will likely be a prank (e.g. substituting one book for another), rather than a serious threat to security. But he says, "Since publishers are rushing to get their delivery product out to everyone, they are really not focusing too much on security of their product, and this will cause future problems."[9]

The Future

So what does the future hold for school libraries? Some may say they are no longer useful. Others, like Beth Holland, believe that while the format may change, the school library will be a "welcoming common space that encourages exploration, creation, and collaboration between students, teachers, and a broader community." It will become a learning hub where the digital and physical resources intersect.[10]

Suzie Boss believes that the media specialist will be a critical member of your project-based learning team. There is a logical connection between the specialist's knowledge of related project resources and expertise that will improve the quality of the project outcome. "Visit schools where project-based learning (PBL) is taking hold and you are almost certain to see teachers collaborating. They may be meeting face-to-face to plan projects, using critical-friend protocols to improve projects, looking at student work together, or even teaming up virtually with project partners in other time zones.

A key player to invite into these collaborative conversations is the school librarian or library media specialist."[11]

PRACTICE

To date Taylor County Schools has been unable to convert completely to a digital library. Tana Penn, the library/media specialist at the high school and an e-library advocate says it is just too expensive to convert an existing collection to digital. She does hasten to add that the students rarely if ever check out the non-fiction books because the Internet provides a more current resource. For Penn the e-library is a way to expand the media center beyond its four walls and make the collection available 24/7.

The TCS e-library is managed by two entities. The Kentucky Virtual Library, a service of the Kentucky Council on Post-Secondary Education in Frankfort, gives TCS students access to eight different web-hosted research sites. OverDrive, a digital content web host headquartered in Cleveland, Ohio, provides the students access to a digital fiction library on line.

Two years prior to Roger Cook being hired as superintendent of Taylor County Schools, Penn discovered OverDrive, but as a small school district representative she found it difficult to get their attention. When she finally got a returned phone call she began plotting how to implement the service in a district whose high school technology consisted of two computer labs in the media center. The purchase of e-readers in addition to the digital library service just was not feasible.

Things changed drastically when Cook came to TCS. Now, not only were students able to bring their cell phones to class, but they were also actually permitted to use them. This one change gave every student with a cell phone access to the proposed digital library. Although she admits that the most usage comes from the high school, the cost of the service is split equally among the schools, as is the yearly cost of acquiring additional titles.

Once the service was in place, a report from the digital service provider (part of the vendor's service) listed over 700 books per month that were being borrowed from the OverDrive account. The majority of these books were being checked out after hours and on weekends. The board and Cook agreed to fund another 15,000 dollars for additional book purchases. Since its inception, the virtual library has been funded for almost 40,000 dollars of purchases. The first books purchased for the e-library were works of fiction. Eventually, biographies and non-fiction works were added. There are 2,609 titles in the collection.

The TCHS media center includes over 15,000 volumes in its collection. The reference material has been eliminated because it was difficult to keep up to date, and it was rarely if ever used. The Kentucky Virtual Library provides research resources to the students, as well as tips on the reliability of the source material currently at a cost of 1,700 dollars per year to TCS.

How Do the e-Libraries Work?

Every student receives a log-in and a password. This gives them access to the e-library (OverDrive) and Kentucky Virtual Library sites on any device.

In OverDrive each book in the collection for the district is catalogued. High school students have access to the entire collection. Middle school students have access to middle and elementary collections. And elementary students can only access the elementary collection. Accelerated learning students can increase their access with a parent's signature. Books are checked out for seven, fourteen or twenty-eight days. If not returned within the requested time, it disappears from the student's list and is available for others to check out. Once a book is checked out, it is not available to another student.

However, a student can put a hold on a book that they would like to read. When the book becomes available, they are notified by e-mail and have up to 24 hours to respond and check the book out. If they do not respond, the book is placed back into the collection and is available to the other students.

The Kentucky Virtual Library, a database for student research, is a curated resource containing multiple sources of information including many historical documents and eight different hosted applications. Here there is a term limit for many of the books in the collection. The purchaser can buy a specific book for one year or many years. Of course the term is reflected in the cost.

Some publishers limit the number of checkouts of a specific volume (e.g. Harper Collins' digital books can only be checked out 26 times before they must be re-purchased). Penn says she originally had an issue with that and did not purchase Harper Collins material as a result. It took her a while to eventually change her mind. Harper Collins publishes many of the books that her students wanted to read and she knows that publishing cannot be done for free. She also reasons that she has to replace hard copies when they wear out, so there's not much difference.

Advantages to an e-Library

There are many advantages to using an e-library including the ability to change the size of the font for easy readability on any device. Once a student selects a book, they receive immediate access. Once the media specialist purchases a book for the collection, it is immediately available to the students. There are no fines to levy for overdue books. Books are not damaged by usage. There is an app available for sight-impaired students. The site is user-friendly and curated by the vendor.

This is the list of top advantages of the e-library from the survey of TCS students:

1. Private—don't have to worry about scary Internet users
2. Portable—Can take it on vacation
3. More books
4. Can change the fonts
5. Saves our Amazon gift cards
6. Paperless—Saves trees

7. No germs
8. 24/7 access—We can check them out in our pajamas
9. No bulky books in our backpacks
10. Don't have to wait for delivery
11. Forces us to finish

Penn also said that since the boys in particular do not want to be seen reading, the e-library is a great way for them to read. They can read on their smartphones, and it is socially acceptable to be seen using your phone.

Maintenance of the collection is another distinct advantage of the e-library. The Taylor County High School collection has been attacked by everything from termites (twenty books were destroyed) to tobacco juice. And the continual use of printed material causes deterioration due to wear and tear. The e-library books are like new for the first reader and the twenty-fifth reader. There is no reduction in quality. If there is an electronic glitch, it is corrected by the vendor.

The other advantage of a curated collection is the record-keeping. TCS is a system that runs on data, and the media centers are no exception. With OverDrive they get a report that tells them what volumes are being accessed, when they are being checked out, and the frequency of use. From this data they know that high school students are the majority of the users. They use the e-library at all hours of the day and night, and they have the highest usage of any small school district in the country. In the district there are 1,387 different OverDrive users. The uses and advantages of the e-library are promoted heavily at the high school. This may be the reason for the highest usage being at that level.

Cost

The cost of an e-library is not only the cost of the curated site and the volumes, but also the cost of the devices needed for access. Since Roger Cook allows his students to have and use their phones in school and has a 1:1 device initiative, access is not an issue at TCS. Tana Penn attempted to initiate an e-library program prior to Mr. Cook's arrival, but said the lack of electronic devices for the students and the logistics of acquiring them exclusively for the library made an e-library unfeasible.

The Kentucky Virtual Library costs TCS 1,700 dollars annually. The OverDrive subscription is available in various tiers. Taylor County Schools is in the 6,000 students or less category and is currently charged 5,999 dollars per year. That cost is paid equally by the three schools. Half of the cost is for the service (technology and curation) and the other half is required for the purchase of additional digital copies (selected by each school's media specialist). Beyond the required minimum annual purchase, the district can purchase as much additional digital material as they are willing to fund. However, in addition to the first cost, they must take into account the term for which a book is purchased for it may need to be renewed. That will also use some of the budget of the required minimum annual purchase account.

What Is Next?

Many school districts are beginning to convert to digital libraries for their entire media collections. Greenville County Schools in South Carolina has already built four schools without a media center. Tana Penn would like to do the same at the new high school building in Taylor County, but is not sure that everyone is ready for that.

A complete conversion to a digital library is costly and is generally done as part of a capital construction project with funds set aside for the new building. The savings from constructing less square footage, not buying the shelving for the books, and not buying the hard copies would almost pay the start-up costs of a digital library. As more and more media specialists struggle to keep their collections current within reduced budgets and less hard copies are checked out by the students, e-libraries will no doubt become more prevalent.

This is not the demise of the media specialist, but rather a change in the tools used. As Tana Penn points out sooner or later everything changes, and you must adapt. And those that enthusiastically adapt, enjoy and flourish.

NOTES

1. Scott, Leslie, and Jeffrey Owings. *School Library Media Centers: Results from the Educational Longitudinal Study of 2002* (ELS: 2002). Washington: National Center for Educational Statistics, 2004.

2. Scott, Leslie, and Jeffrey Owings. *School Library Media Centers: Results from the Educational Longitudinal Study of 2002* (ELS: 2002). Ibid.

3. Piketty, Thomas. *Capital in the 21st Century.* Cambridge: The President and Fellows of Harvard College, 2014.

4. Lance, Keith Curry, Marcia J. Rodney, and Christine Hamilton-Pennell. *Powerful Libraries Make Powerful Students.* Canton: Illinois School Library Media Association, 2005.

5. Rodney, Marcia J., Keith Curry Lance, and Christine Hamilton-Pennell. *The Impact of Michigan School Librarians on Academic Achievement: Kids who Have Libraries Succeed.* Lansing: Library of Michigan, 2003.

6. School Library Journal. "SLJ's Average Book Prices 2014." *School Library Journal.* March 31, 2014. www.slj.com/2014/03/research/sljs-average-book-prices-2014/ (accessed February 14, 2015).

7. North Carolina Department of Instruction. "IMPACT: Guidelines for Media and Technology Programs." North Carolina Public Schools. January 2008. http://www.ncpublicschools.org_docs_dtl_resources_impact_8collection_guidelines.pdf (accessed February 22, 2015).

8. Penn, Tana, interview by Michael Raible. Librarian/Media Specialist at Taylor County High School (February 24, 2015).

9. Brown, Bill, interview by Michael K. Raible. Executive Director, Education Technology Services, Greenvile County Schools, Greenville, SC (February 22, 2015).

10. Holland, Beth. "21st-Century Libraries: The Learning Commons." *Edutopia*. January 14, 2015. www.edutopia.org/blog/21st-century-libraries-learning-commons-beth-holland (accessed June 15, 2015).

11. Boss, Suzie. "Are School Librarians Part of Your PBL Dream Team?" *Edutopia*. October 28, 2013. http://www.edutopia.org/blog/school-librarians-part-pbl-team-dream-suzie-boss (accessed June 15, 2015).

SIX

Early Release Fridays for Professional Development

"I am often asked about how I got the community to buy in to sending students home early on Fridays. Thing is, I never asked. I gave the parents and students an alternative, and at first many students stayed at school on Friday for additional tutoring. But now, it is unusual to have more than 10 percent of our students stay in school on early release days." —Roger Cook

THEORY

Education is a continuous improvement process. While students are learning more about content, teachers are learning more about how to teach. Much of the focus in K–12 education has been on the student learner and the resulting academic outcomes. However, without a parallel concentration on the educators and their acquisition of better teaching skills, improvement will be elusive at best. While most K–12 institutions believe in giving students many opportunities to learn, they often find it difficult to provide similar advantages to their teachers.

The majority of educational reform literature exhorts district human relations professionals to hire and retain the best. The October 28, 2010 issue of the *American Society of Curriculum Developers (ASCD) Express* entitled, *Hiring and Retaining Good Teachers,* is but one example.[1] Effective teaching by and large is seen as a "gift," practiced in the isolation of the classroom, and not something to be learned either through training or collaboration.

Richard Elmore believes that the reason most education reform does not reach the technical core (the classroom) is that a "loose-coupling" between administrative functions and teaching exists and has buffered what occurs in the classroom. "The theory of loose-coupling explains why schools continue to promote structures and to engage in practices that research and experience suggest are manifestly not productive for the learning of certain students."[2]

Taylor County Schools are very careful to point out that the two hour early release on every Friday is for improving teaching and learning. This time is specifically scheduled and protected for meetings of the professional learning communities and for the review and analysis of student data among the teachers and administrators.

Vanessa Vega, former senior manager of research at Edutopia, says there are three keys to successful professional development: effective administrator and teacher leadership, job-embedded professional development, and professional development communities.[3]

Experience

In one of his essays on professional development, Elmore, a professor at the Harvard Graduate School of Education says, "The prevailing assumption is that teachers learn most of what they need to know about how to teach before they enter the classroom—despite massive evidence to the contrary—and that most of what they learn after they begin teaching falls into the amorphous category of 'experience.'"[4]

Teacher experience with various means and methods of instructional delivery is a process of trial and error—finding techniques that show promise and discarding those that do not. But teacher experience, because of the day-to-day demands on time, often becomes routine with little opportunity for experimentation or access to other methods. Formal professional development allows teachers to acquire new skills and ideas about content delivery. It is virtually the only means of changing instructional practices that will ultimately lead to the improvement of academic outcomes.

Professional Development

Much of the criticism from today's teaching professionals is that staff development is perfunctory—activities to fill the hours of teacher workdays required to be built into the calendar for the school year, but not really useful or applicable to each and every staff member. Often the time in professional development is spent on improving attitude, since high expectations have been found to be one element of better outcomes.

Thomas R. Guskey, professor at the College of Education at the University of Kentucky provides an interesting perspective on the sequence of professional development. His research has been on the theory that instructional practice changes attitude. He says that the sequence should be professional development for skills and practices that have demonstrated success in changing outcomes. As the students show progress with the use of these methods of practice, teacher attitudes and expectations change. Successful practice changes beliefs.[5]

In order to be effective and change outcomes, staff development must focus on real students with real problems in real surroundings. "Professional development is the set of knowledge- and skill-building activities that raise the capacity of teachers and administrators to respond to external demands and to engage in the improvement of practice and performance."[6]

It is important to note that effective professional development builds the skills to improve the educational corps, it is not an individual exercise. Quality staff development deals with skills and pedagogy that contribute to organizational performance. This is not a resume enhancement, but a deepening of instructional capacity within the district.

Reciprocity

If the purpose of professional development is the improvement of instructional outcomes, then in this age of accountability it must also be reciprocal. For every uptick in performance that is expected, there is an equal responsibility to invest in providing capacity in the skills and pedagogy to create the uptick. For every staff development investment there must be an equal commitment on the part of those being trained to improve performance.[7] As is often the case, the reciprocal agreement is not fulfilled when the quality of the investment is inferior or when academic performance does not meet the expectation.

In order for the reciprocal agreement to function and be of lasting value, specific high quality training in skills and pedagogy must be provided. Professional development must address specific issues in a local context.

Culture

Continuous improvement through professional development is a community effort, a culture of improvement, not a position description. Professional development, whether in a smaller district or a larger school district must be a group effort. Everyone must be involved. Part of the incentive is the recognition of effort by the community when something doesn't work, as well as the recognition of success when it does.

Time

One of the most difficult aspects of providing quality staff development is the time it takes to develop and deliver. During the school year teachers and administrators are continuously involved in the delivery of content to students. It is rare to have any time during the school year for teacher and administrator training. Since school districts are often not penalized for a school day that is truncated, some school districts use an early release day to set aside time for development. Other districts build additional "seat time" into their schedules to allow for some early release professional development time.

Several North Carolina school districts have experimented with some form of early release. Chapel Hill-Carrboro City Schools does an early release on one Thursday every month. Iredell-Statesville Schools has six early release staff development days on the calendar and Charlotte-Mecklenburg Schools plan four early release days in the 2015–2016 school year.

At Sarah Cobb Elementary School in Americus, Georgia, students are released one hour early one day a week. The school exceeds the minimum number of instructional minutes required by the state in order to do so. Since most of the schools exceed the minimum required seat time mandated by the State of Washington, the Snoqualmie School District has early release days on Fridays for professional development.

Classes start thirty minutes late and teachers arrive thirty minutes early on Wednesdays at Holtville High School in Holtville, California. So teachers get one hour every Wednesday morning for collaborative planning in their study groups. At Boyle County Schools in Kentucky, students are dismissed two hours early every Wednesday in September, October, March, and April to allow teachers some professional development time.

However, early release schedules are not without their complexities. Transportation, child care, student activities, negotiated employment agreements, and state regulations regarding "seat time" must also be considered. In late 2009 much to the chagrin of the local teachers association, the Wake County North Carolina Board of Education eliminated their regular early release "Wacky Wednesdays" because they said they were too controversial.

PRACTICE

Taylor County Schools releases students two hours early every Friday of the school year for the purpose of staff development. Performance-based education is a process that is deep into data review and analysis. The two hours each week devoted to professional learning is considered to be the minimum necessary. Roger Cook admits he would like to provide more time for professional development.

Logistics

Each school in Taylor County is released at 1:00 pm. The small contingent of classified staff at each school assists with traffic duty and other assignments to allow the certified staff to begin their development at 1:15 or 1:20. Bus transportation is provided for students at the early dismissal. There is no late bus.

Each school is on a seven period day. Those seven periods are truncated on Fridays into roughly thirty minutes apiece. All three principals agree this is not wasted time. With some judicious planning solid content is delivered on Fridays, just like it is every other day of the week.

Lunch time is a little more complex, since it isn't scheduled at the usual middle period on Fridays. "But we make it work," says Laura Benningfield, the principal for the high school.

The professional learning communities (PLC's) at each school are configured differently. At the high school, since the grade levels are less distinct, the professional learning communities are formed around content (some would call this departmental). At the middle school there are both content and grade level PLC's, but those that deal with content tend to meet more frequently. Just as in the high school, the grade levels are more fluid. At the elementary school, although there are content and grade level professional learning communities. The grade levels are more distinct, so the PLC's that meet most often are grade level and not content-based.

This time is also not used for staff meetings. Each principal uses technology to keep their staff informed and while a few minutes are used for "housekeeping items," those are held to a minimum. Sometimes Cook will use technology to inform the entire staff of a new program or to provide an explanation of an issue. In that case the staffs of all three schools are asked to assemble in the media centers, and the superintendent will present and entertain questions from "the big board" in his office.

Planning

While some departmental or grade level planning is accomplished during early release Fridays the concentration is on professional development and data analysis. Teachers are given individual planning time during each school day. Mr. Cook is quick to admit that he would like to give his staff more time for planning and training. "This is hard work and there is just not enough time. I wish we could do early release every day."

Agendas for each early release are prepared in advance by each school principal and submitted to district leadership in case there is a desire to participate. Rarely is there a need to revise the agenda because of input or editing from leadership. Since administrators and district leadership cannot attend every workshop every Friday, an electronic attendance form is used to report which training each staff member attended.

In-house expertise is especially useful for training during early release days. For example, there are two Taylor County teachers that have become very proficient in project-based instructional delivery. These teachers have been making the rounds at various PLC's and schools to help the other staff become more comfortable with this methodology and to provide examples of how they have approached this delivery method.

Required Attendance

Each principal stresses the importance of staff attendance at each early release day. This is not a time for teachers to do errands or leave the school for personal business. The logistics are in place to make sure that each and every staff member is duty free and able to attend. A request for absence must be approved by the superintendent.

Alternatives for Students

There are alternatives for students who are unable to go home early on Fridays. Those students whose parents are unable to arrange for them to go to a supervised location after school can attend additional tutoring sessions in the 1:00 pm to 3:00 pm time slot. These sessions are taught by the few classified staff members.

While initially there were about 10 percent of the students that took advantage of these sessions, the number has dwindled over time. There are currently about fifty elementary students that stay in school on Fridays and many less at the middle and high schools. Bus transportation is provided for the early release students. Parents must pick up or provide transportation for those students that remain until 3:00.

Teamwork

Roger Cook has said, "I guess a team that didn't practice together might still win a few games, but if you really want a championship team you have to practice. And that's what early release Fridays are for—our team of teachers."

Every principal mentioned the relationship building among their staffs as a positive result of the early release days. "We are a family. We work hard together, we celebrate together, and we solve our problems together," says Tony Jewell, TCS middle school principal.

With student success as the purpose, every teacher is hungry to learn techniques to improve outcomes. But every teacher has a different personality and often a different approach to learning. Meeting regularly in the professional learning communities engages the staff in the common purpose. This is not a district in which teachers develop their expertise in isolation.

So when do the conversations occur about individual students? "Mostly during the work day," says Laura Benningfield. Counselors and teachers discuss those issues when they meet in the hallways, at lunch, or during a pre-arranged meeting before, during, or after school. This is true at the high school because the PLC's are organized by content. Some of those discussions do occur on Fridays at the elementary and middle levels in the grade level professional learning communities.

Professional Development

The distributed leadership model means that professional development at Taylor County Schools is not a staff position; it is everyone's job. If you have learned a new way to enhance literacy, you share it. If your class has not understood time and motion in physics, you ask for help. Every teacher has successes and failures. This is not about individual accolades, instead it is all about coaching and sharing with your PLC to increase expertise for the entire team.

There are times when the entire teaching corps in a school meets to learn about something. With the *Race to the Top* federal funding, the elementary school staff was able to begin professional development that included *The Leader in Me* program. This program developed by Stephen R. Covey uses *The Seven Habits of Highly Effective People* as a common terminology and integrates leadership development into everything that is done in the school.

Recently at the high school, the topic was the six spokes of performance-based education. This is a work in progress, a relatively new concept for the district. Eventually each course will be characterized by its method of delivery. And that will be identified in the material that the students use to begin to register in January for their classes for the following school year.

As each student meets with a counselor or principal, they will be able to rely upon the written material to decide which courses are best for them, instead of relying upon the administrator's knowledge of each of the courses and how they are taught.

Roger Cook's three rules are: (1) no child fails, (2) no one is held back because of their age, and (3) no one drops out. The staff were asked if those three rules created any additional pressure on them. To a person they all answered no. They explained that these were all things that every teacher wants. Being accountable for them was really not a big deal.

Cook believes the lessons he learned as a football coach have served him well in district leadership. "A coach might know how every position should be played, but he can't play any of them." Distributed leadership and a belief that staff development is everyone's job are the keys.

Tony Jewell, the middle school principal said, "Without early release Fridays we couldn't do performance-based education like we have. It takes that kind of commitment to professional development to make it work."

In the *Knowing-Doing Gap* Jeffrey Pfeffer and Robert I. Sutton say that organizations often substitute memory for thinking. "The organization's memory embodied in precedents, customs of unknown origin, stories about how things have always been and used to be, and standard operating procedures, becomes used as a substitute for taking wise action."[8] Roger Cook had the advantage of beginning his own traditions. He said, "Education as we have known it is dead." The difficult work that goes on in Taylor County Schools during early release Fridays has made that a reality.

NOTES

1. "Hiring and Retaining Good Teachers." ASCD Express, 2010
2. Elmore, Richard F. *School Reform from the Inside Out*. Cambridge: Harvard University Press, 2004.
3. Vega, Vanessa. "Teacher Development Research Review: Keys to Educator Success." *Edutopia*. January 3, 2013. www.edutopia.org/teacher-development-research-keys-success (accessed June 19, 2015).
4. Elmore, Richard F. *School Reform from the Inside Out*. Ibid.
5. Guskey, Thomas R. "Professional Development and Teacher Change." *Teachers and Teaching: Theory and Practice*, 2002: 381–91.
6. Elmore, Richard F. *School Reform from the Inside Out*. Ibid.
7. Elmore, Richard F. *School Reform from the Inside Out*. Ibid.
8. Pfeffer, Jeffrey, and Robert I. Sutton. *The Knowing-Doing Gap*. Cambridge: Harvard Business School Publishing, 2000.

SEVEN
Ubiquitous Technology

"I think there is a world market for maybe five computers." —Thomas Watson, Chairman of International Business Machines, 1943

THEORY

Since education is risk-averse, new instructional tools are always greeted with some degree of skepticism and technology is certainly no exception. Some of the hesitation to include technology into the spectrum of education was because it had a variety of uses.

Computer labs in high schools replaced the rooms of typewriters as "keyboarding" or data input was initially viewed as another skill to be acquired by those students in the secretarial or business support classes. The computer labs at the elementary and middle levels were used to drill students on content—in math initially and then in reading.

As devices and software became more sophisticated and technology became a status symbol, administrators lobbied for three or more devices in each classroom in addition to a computer lab. They felt this was a way to demonstrate that their school was up to date with the latest instructional trends since access to the computer lab was limited. (A student in a school of 500 students might be lucky to have one hour a week in the lab.) Teacher training on the devices usually from a member of the faculty was also limited. As a result, teaching that blended traditional delivery methods with technology progressed very slowly.

With the introduction of the net book in late 2007, an easily portable low-cost device that relied upon wireless access to programs, educators began to discuss the possibility of putting a device in the hands of every student. School districts began looking at wireless access within each school not as an amenity, but as a necessity.

Although an inexpensive and portable device is one-third of the issue, user-friendly software is another third. In 2010 Apple unveiled the iPad. Since then, the number of software applications (apps) has grown exponentially. In April of 2010 there were 3,000 apps available for the iPad. By July 2012 that number was 200,000 and recently Apple announced that there were over one million apps available online. The availability of software no longer appears to be a problem.

The other issue, the training of teachers, still lags behind the development of hardware and software. Cited by many experts as the main reason for the slow pace of integration of technology into education, staff development is underfunded and often overlooked as a critical element of blended learning.

Not everyone is convinced that computers have a place in the classroom. Larry Cuban, Emeritus Professor at the Stanford Graduate School of Education, is more than a little suspicious about the Silicon Valley connection to the school reform movement. A view he expresses in his 2001 book, *Oversold and Underused: Computers in the Classroom*.

He argues that the hyper-investment in technology should be predicated on the broader notion of the social and civic goals we are trying to accomplish through public education. If technology can enhance these efforts, then perhaps the investment is worthwhile. But we must first agree as to the purpose of education and "without a broader vision of the social and civic role that school perform in a democratic society, our current excessive focus on technology use in schools runs the danger of trivializing our nation's core ideals."[1]

Incorporating Technology into Teaching

In his article titled, *If Not Here, Where? Understanding Teacher's Use of Technology in Silicon Valley Schools*, Pedro Hernández-Ramos explains that even in the cradle of electronic civilization teachers alone do not control whether or not their students have access to the latest technology. Teachers even in Silicon Valley do not control teacher preparation, administrator knowledge of software applications, access to technical support or budget control, all of which are also factors in technology integration into the classroom.[2]

Abigail Garthwaite and Herman G. Weller were in the middle of the Maine Learning Technology Initiative (MLTI). Their research involved following two middle school teachers (Susan and Rick) as they went through the first year of MLTI. During the fall of 2002 more than 17,000 seventh graders and their teachers were given Apple laptop computers at the beginning of the school year. Each i-book had word-processing, e-mail and Internet capabilities, and *The World Book Encyclopedia*.[3]

Both teachers were well-qualified, having taken graduate level courses in the application of technology. Since prior to the laptops, their teaching styles were different, their approaches to using the technology for content were also different. Susan used the technology as supplemental content. "When teaching, Susan's typical communication dynamic was a hub-to-spoke pattern, with the teacher mediating the discussion and interactions. She typically began with lengthy and detailed explanations of the topic, interspersing question and answer time with generous portions of seatwork."[4]

Rick began his lessons with a brief introduction and then allowed his students to pursue the answers to the assignment through written material, Internet material on a web site that he prepared and on the Internet in general. "Much of the students' learning came from collecting and interacting with their own data and in discussions with team members about processing this information."[5]

Susan ended the year ambivalent about the use of the laptops. She saw the advantages of keeping some of her students engaged, but just wasn't comfortable turning over some of the basic instruction to technology. Rick felt the laptops had changed his life. He felt the laptops engaged the students more easily in independent learning.

"For both teachers, the effects of ubiquitous computing were strongly shaped by their beliefs about teaching and learning."[6] Maine's year of the laptops (now called the Maine Learning Technology Initiative) did not automatically change instructional delivery from teacher-centered to student-centered, but it did and continues to put technology into the hands of every seventh grade student in the state. The program was recently modified to replace those devices in the beginning of the freshman year in high school.

Vanessa Vega cites four meta-analyses that indicate that blended learning (i.e. a combination of face-to-face teacher time and online learning) produces better results than online learning alone. Her review of the research also found "successful technology integration for learning generally goes hand in hand with changes in teacher training, curricula, and assessment practices." In her review she cites three principles common to successful technology integration:

- Students active in learning and getting frequent, personalized feedback
- Critical student analysis of and creation of media messages
- Connecting learning to the world outside the classroom[7]

Outcomes

Kathleen Debevec and her co-authors were curious about outcomes for students in technology-integrated classrooms.[8] In their research they divided seventy-nine undergraduate college students into four groups based upon their learning preferences: preferred technology use and not traditional methodology, preferred traditional methodology and not technology, high preference for both, or low preference for both.

They expected that technology would be a valuable learning tool, but not a substitute for class attendance. They also expected that preference for one instructional methodology over another would not affect outcomes. While the use of the technology and the associated material enhanced understanding of the course content, it was class attendance that was most closely associated with better student performance. Preference for one method over another did not preclude students from using the additional material (PowerPoint slides and related videos) to study for their exams and prepare for class. Most students took full advantage of all the material.

Students who preferred technology use and not traditional methodology, or preferred traditional methodology and not technology had the best class attendance and the highest exam performance. Those students with a high preference for both methodologies, or low preference for both did not perform as well and both groups had the lowest class attendance.

The researchers concluded based upon previous research that class attendance was a significant factor because the computer-assisted presentations and multimedia used in the classroom helped students remember what they were learning, enhanced their interest in learning the subject, and improved their understanding of course material.

In 2008 Chrystalla Mouza studied 1:1 laptop initiative in one of fifty-two schools located in an urban New York City school district. Approximately 94 percent of the students were economically disadvantaged students (eligible for free or reduced price lunches). The goal of the program, *Microsoft Anytime, Anywhere, Learning*, was to increase access to technology and to begin to bridge the digital divide.

"As this work demonstrated, ubiquitous access to technology and access to well-prepared teachers who value the experiences that technology offers can help ensure equality of digital opportunities among less advantaged students."[9]

The results of this study demonstrated how access to technology assisted well-prepared educators in creating activities that gave students a chance to think, write, create, and develop meaningful projects. Qualitative data in the study seemed to indicate that students who had access to laptops produced academic gains in areas such as writing and mathematics.

Pedagogy

Over forty years ago M.I.T. professor Seymour Papert said, "The phrase 'technology and education' usually means inventing new gadgets to teach the same old stuff in a thinly disguised version of the same old way. Moreover, if the gadgets are computers, the teaching becomes incredibly more expensive and biased towards its dullest parts, namely the kind of rote learning in which measurable results can be obtained by treating the children like pigeons in a Skinner box."[10]

Technology may provide a pathway, but is not necessarily transformative. Papert is a strong advocate for a 1:1 educational environment in which each student has his or her own device. But just as structure does not change pedagogy, so too the introduction of technology does not automatically create a student-centered environment. Deep changes to educational delivery occur as a result of visionary leadership and clearly stated instructional goals, not because every student and teacher has access to a computer.

As we have seen in the earlier example pedagogy must change to take full advantage of access to technology. A fully-blended learning experience will include individual work on assignments as well as work in groups. Content areas that would seem to be able to benefit the most from access to current information (history, civics, geography) have been some of the slowest to fully integrate technology. Content areas with little variation in day-to-day content (math, science, etc.) have typically been faster to adopt. Which indicates that the issue may be the quality and reliability of content, and not necessarily comfort with instructional technology.

Professional Development

Virtually all of the research articles on the inclusion and integration of technology into the classroom mention educators that are well prepared. As mentioned elsewhere in this book, teacher preparation (pre-service and in-service) is critical to the success of a blended learning program. Nita Matzen and Julie Edmunds speculate in their research that much of teachers' professional development concentrates on skills, not pedagogy.[11]

"An inherent flaw in the design of skills-based technology professional development is that the focus is not on instructional practices. When teachers are provided with technology professional development focusing primarily on technical skills, they may fall back on technology uses consistent with their existing instructional practices simply because they have not been provided with an alternative vision for the use of technology."[12]

The dilemma here is that if the technology training does not show the educator how to incorporate its use into their delivery method, they may forego the use of the computer, believing it does not support the way they teach. Since teachers select methodology based upon what has been successful in the past. So it is not just skills training that is required, but an explanation for how to incorporate the use of technology into their personal instructional delivery protocol.

Technical Support

There is a saying in the educational facilities business that there is nothing more useless than a new school that is completed in mid-October. Likewise there is little more useless than a computer that will not work on the day a lesson has been planned that integrates technology. That computer might as well be a paperweight.

Technical support in the technology environment is necessary. And it must be bigger than a break-fix protocol. If a device does not operate, another must be on hand to replace it. If the connectivity is disrupted, another access point must be available. If the software is corrupted, an alternative must be created. In each of these cases it is not just the fix, it is the timeliness of the repair that is the difference between success and failure.

Myths

Andrew Marcinek and Karla Evers discuss the various myths related to 1:1 technology integration in their blog on the Edutopia web site. Evers is an English teacher at Grafton High School in Massachusetts and Marcinek has learned about 1:1 initiatives first hand at the intersection of myth and reality when iPads were introduced into his classroom four years ago. "Over the last four years, I've noticed several trends and themes that have surrounded the iPad—most notably, that the device itself was a driving force in classroom instruction. This could not be further from the truth."

They say the devices should be viewed as supplemental and not primary to teaching and learning. The technology allows a teacher to challenge students in new ways. It revises the teacher's role to that of facilitator of learning. "The best approach for teachers is to plan and design their lessons at the intersection of instruction and technology. And sometimes the technology won't even need to be planned—it will just naturally occur. The key, despite the technology involved, is to challenge students and provoke their learning by making the device necessary and meaningful to solving a problem or developing a solution."[13]

PRACTICE

Technology is everywhere in Taylor County Schools. In addition to the workstations in the virtual academy, every student is allowed to bring their own device (BYOD). Cell phones can be used. And Cook eventually wants to make sure every student has a tablet or laptop. Currently high school students have Lenovo *Yoga*'s. This is a small laptop with a detachable touchscreen display. The fourth through eighth grades have iPads. Many of the kindergarten through third grades have some devices in their classroom, but they are not yet at one-to-one. Every teacher has been provided with a desktop computer and an iPad at the elementary and middle schools and a Yoga at the high school.

History

When Roger Cook was hired by Taylor County Schools in 2009, the district had just begun a project to install wireless access points in the schools. There was not a BYOD or one-to-one initiative. There were no computers in the classrooms. The teachers did all of their work on paper.

The week before school started a stack of papers about a foot tall arrived on the superintendent's desk. "What's this?" he asked. He was told that each teacher was required to prepare a lesson plan for the week and these were the teacher's plans for the first week of school. "Teachers have more important things to do with their time," he said and threw the stack in the wastebasket.

The first iPads were issued to all of the high school students in 2012. They were third generation devices with thirty-two gigabytes of memory. The selection was based upon application availability, the ability to personalize the educational programs, and battery life. Leased from Apple without a protection plan or insurance, TCS soon developed a plan to charge, synchronize, and repair the iPads in house.

Since the Apple charging stations were too expensive, the TCS maintenance department built the racks for charging the devices. Two ten-port USB hubs and a MacBook were used to sync the devices, another function of the Apple carts, in order to install additional software. (Students do not have administrative rights on the machines, so software must be installed by the district.) Staff and eventually students were certified as Apple repair technicians and found a source for wholesale replacement parts. ITC Tech runs out of a classroom at the high school with staff and students providing technical support.

In 2014 the iPads were sent to grades four through eight, and the Yogas were distributed to every high school student. This time TCS bought the damage repair plan as part of the package, but they are working on a plan to become a certified repair shop so that the time for a device to be out of service can be minimized. ITC Tech still acts as technical support and still charges the devices that remain at school.

IPad technical support had to occur at the middle school as well as the high school, so a branch of ITC Tech was opened at the middle school. Run by middle school students, it is also an iPad charging and repair station. The elementary school tablets are charged and synced on carts in the classrooms overnight. System Center Configuration Manager (SCCM) functionality from Microsoft now allows the district to push software out to each device.

Major upgrades and expansion to wireless access have occurred in the schools. Two new schools are under construction in the district, and it is anticipated that wireless coverage in those facilities will be universal. About half of the school bus fleet also has WiFi.

At last check, there were over 800 devices using the district's guest wireless network.

Access

Roughly 18 percent of students do not have access at home to a network that is robust enough to allow video streaming. Some areas of the county do not have reliable cell phone service. This is an issue of topography and residential density making it unfeasible economically for a provider to make high speed Internet or cell coverage available.

Since streaming access may be a problem for some students, one of the selection criteria for devices has been that they have to be able to download content. Most students save to their personal drive on the district server or to the cloud. Either situation allows the students access to their material should something happen that takes their device out of service. In that case the student is provided a loaner device until theirs is fixed.

Device Distribution

There are three ways for a student in Taylor County Schools to receive a device from the district:

1. Personal Plan: Student will bring her/his personal iPad or Yoga to school for use in their daily activities. Student will be responsible for the device and join the guest wireless network at school. (Students can have their devices updated with apps through the school if they choose to do so.)
2. Lease Plan: Student will lease an iPad or Yoga from the school district by either paying a 200 dollar fee or by selling 200 dollars' worth of fundraising tickets as provided by the school. The tickets and money from the tickets must be returned to the school by the posted date in order for the sales to be eligible. The student will be allowed to take the iPad or Yoga home, returning it to the school as requested for updates, maintenance and application installation. By doing so the student will be earning credit toward the eventual purchase of the iPad or Yoga. A protective case will be provided for the device.
3. School Plan: Student will NOT participate in the 1:1 iPad or Yoga initiative. They could have access to a device while at school as needed for instructional purposes. These devices are returned every day to the classroom cart for recharging.

As part of the lease program Taylor County Schools provides and administers an insurance program for students and parents as part of the iPad and Yoga implementation. The plan covers "accidental" damage to the device and is designed to limit the family's financial responsibility for most accidental damage.

The fundraising tickets in Option 2 are part of an arrangement with a local appliance dealer. The retailer donates appliances or electronics for the raffle. A 70" television was raffled last year. The tickets are sold at ten dollars apiece. If the student is able to sell twenty tickets, their annual commitment is fulfilled and they are given the use of a device for an entire year. This is just another way that TCS tries to balance the equity issue.

BYOD

Much has been made of the security and structure of access for devices that are purchased and brought to school by individual students. Cook is somewhat cavalier about the issue. "Students will find a way to use these devices to access sites that are not appropriate. When teachers or administrators see them, they make sure they stop."

TCS also uses LanSchool, a classroom technology management software that can show a teacher what each student in their classroom has on their screen.

Bryan Cook, the TCS Chief Information Officer, says the biggest challenge with BYOD is making sure that the student experience is consistent. The only requirements are that the device has anti-virus software, that it supports whatever software the teacher is using, and that it has sufficient battery power to run the device through the entire school day.

Participation

Teachers are using the technology to advantage for participation in content when a student is absent due to illness or offering assistance when not in class. Taylor County was the first district in Kentucky to develop what they call cyber snow days. It was one of the waivers they requested from the Kentucky Department of Education as part of their designation as a District of Innovation.

A packet of material goes home with the students in the late fall or early winter. That packet contains five days' worth of lessons. When Cook announces that school must be closed due to inclement weather, the students attend school through technology. Over 98 percent of the students turn in their work on cyber snow days.

Security

The district is currently researching a tracking program that will identify the location of a device from its signal. Loss of devices due to theft or carelessness has not been a big problem at TCS, but the Chief Information Officer wants to be prepared.

All materials that are put into the devices (removable drives, etc.) are all scanned prior to use. The security and periodic revision of teachers' identifications and passwords are their individual responsibility. To date there have been no incidents.

Teleconferencing

The district is set up to do teleconferencing via Skype. As teachers and administrators become more comfortable with this technology, it will no doubt receive increased usage.

The Future

As Bryan Cook thinks about opening the new high school, he would like to initiate a program where every device goes home at the end of the day. "The logistics of collecting the school devices from each class at three o'clock and charging those devices and then putting them on carts for the teachers to collect first thing every morning is a pain."

He expects the tech support and break/fix part of the operation will still exist, but the loading, charging, and unloading of all of the devices is not something he wants to continue once the new high school is built and occupied.

He also expects that the iPads, or a similar device, will eventually make their way into the hands of every elementary school student. That's the superintendent's plan as well. He wants the tools to be able to offer education at every level twenty-four hours a day, seven days a week. And the only way to make that happen is to put a device into the hands of every student.

NOTES

1. Cuban, Larry. *Oversold and Underutilized: Computers in the Classroom.* Cambridge: Harvard University Press, 2001.

2. Hernandez-Ramos, Pedro. "If Not Here Where? Understanding Teacher's Use of Techonolgy in Silicon Valley Schools." *Journal of Research on Technology in Education,* 2005: 39–64.

3. Garthwaite, Abigail, and Herman G. Weller. "A Year in the Life: Two Seventh Grade Teachers Implement One-to-One Computing." *Journal of Reasearch on Technology in Education,* 2005: 361–77.

4. Garthwaite, Abigail, and Herman G. Weller. "A Year in the Life: Two Seventh Grade Teachers Implement One-to-One Computing." *Ibid.*

5. Garthwaite, Abigail, and Herman G. Weller. "A Year in the Life: Two Seventh Grade Teachers Implement One-to-One Computing." *Ibid.*

6. Garthwaite, Abigail, and Herman G. Weller. "A Year in the Life: Two Seventh Grade Teachers Implement One-to-One Computing." *Ibid.*

7. Vega, Vanessa. "Technology Integration Research Review." *Edutopia*. February 5, 2013. http://www.edutopia.org/technology-integration-research-learning-outcomes (accessed June 19, 2015).

8. Debevec, Kathleeen, Meh-Yau Shih, and Vishal Kashyap. "Learning Strategies and Performance in a Tchnology Intergrated Classroom." *Journal of Research on Technology in Education*, 2006: 293–307.

9. Mouza, Chrystalla. "Learning with Laptops: Implementation and Outcomes in an Urban, Under-Pivileged School." *Journal of Research on Technology in Education*, 2008: 447–472.

10. Papert, Seymour. *Teaching Children Thinking*. Memo, Cambridge: Massachusetts Institute of Techonology, 1971.

11. Matzen, Nita, and Julie Edmunds. "Technology as a Catalyst for Change: The Role of Professional Development." *The Journal of Research on Technology in Education*, 2007: 417–430.

12. Matzen, Nita, and Julie Edmunds. "Technology as a Catalyst for Change: The Role of Professional Development." *Ibid.*

13. Marcinek, Andrew, and Karla Evers. "Myth vs. Reality in a 1:1 Classroom." *Edutopia*. May 7, 2015. www.edutopia.org/blog/myth-vs-reality-one-to-one-andrew-marcinek-karla-evers (accessed June 19, 2015).

EIGHT

Career Pathways

"Far and away the best prize that life offers is the chance to work hard at work worth doing." —Theodore Roosevelt

THEORY

The Career Pathways program is an enhanced career and technical education that gives students the chance to sample a career through various courses and hands-on experiences. This is not your typical trade school or vocational school experience. It is exploratory in nature. Students learn both core and electives as applied to a specific career focus.

The Federal Legislation

When the Carl D. Perkins Career and Technical Education Act of 2006 was signed into law, it included some revisions to the former enabling legislation.[1] The first and most obvious was the change in terminology from vocational education to career and technical education. Guidance counselors as well as CTE instructors were included in those responsible for the guidance and student development process. And CTE now included academic, technical, and skill-building responsibilities.

Research

With the strong emphasis today on students being college bound, Marisa Castellano and her co-authors wondered whether career-based education had any effect on post-secondary enrollment. They decided to study high schools with significant at-risk populations that were undergoing comprehensive school reforms. What they found was that participation in a career-based curriculum had no effect on academic achievement, engagement, or transition to post-secondary institutions.[2]

However, students whose coursework was more heavily weighted toward career-based studies were more likely to have a post-secondary plan and were far less likely to drop out of school. This research was done during the changes responding to *No Child Left Behind* and during the re-authorization of the Career and Technical Education Improvement Act of 2006. The authors felt that once the changes were fully implemented, there would be other positive results to report.

An earlier report from Stephen Plank also found that students in the CTE program were less likely to drop out,[3] but the differences in the two reports do point to a changing situation for career and technical education.

Plank divided his students into four categories: academic concentrators, CTE concentrators, dual concentrators, and those that have no concentration of coursework.

He reports that academic achievement and transition to a post-secondary institution were lowest among those students that were CTE concentrators. The highest rate of dropouts was among the concentrators, both academic and CTE. Those students characterized as dual concentrators (taking substantial coursework in academic and CTE) were the least likely to drop out.

In the six years between the first and second reports, a change had occurred for the better in career and technical education. Students in both reports were selected at random, but the results were significantly different. By 2007 CTE was becoming a pathway for career sampling and not just trade school. The variety of courses was increasing and the outcomes reported in the later report reflect that improvement.

Pedagogy

Career and Technical Education has evolved from chiefly a skills-based discipline (auto mechanics, construction trades, agriculture and home economics) to a survey of a broad spectrum of careers through experiential learning.

Over seventy-five years ago John Dewey famously forwarded the theory that experience and reflection lead to true learning—learning that leads to application.[4] In their extensive survey of the literature on experiential learning Dr. Robert Clark, Dr. Mark Threeton, and Dr. John Ewing found that "each model of experiential learning includes some form of experience, reflection, and application. Most importantly each theoretical model of the experiential learning cycle does not 'stop' at the experience which is often characterized by the application of theoretical knowledge learned in a formal educational setting. When learning stops at the experience, it limits the learner's capacity to reflect on the experience and to acquire a deeper understanding from it."[5]

Experiential learning is the basis of CTE. Many students learn far more if they can see the practical application of what they are learning within the context of a career in which they have expressed an interest.

Dropout Prevention

The research indicates that a mix of academic and CTE courses can decrease the dropout rate. In fact, The National Center for Dropout Prevention includes a quality career and technical education program as one of its fifteen strategies that have the most positive impact on the dropout rate.[6]

The positive influences of career and technical education on dropout prevention listed in the report are the following:

- Enhancement of students' motivation and academic achievement;
- Increased personal and social competence related to work in general;
- A broad understanding of an occupation or industry;
- Career exploration and planning; and
- Acquisition of knowledge or skills related to employment in particular occupations or more generic work competencies.[7]

Nationally, the 2014 average graduation rate for those high school students concentrating in CTE is now 93 percent, compared to an average adjusted cohort graduation rate of 80 percent for all high school students.[8]

Benefits for the Students

Work-related education benefits students by applying their academic knowledge to a real world situation. They get to connect what they are learning to a career context. Students get to learn about career possibilities and perhaps even improve their chances for post-graduation employment. They get to develop and practice appropriate development and practice of positive work-related habits and attitudes including critical thinking, problem solving, and teamwork. Through career experience students can network for future employment, expand and refine their technical skills, and observe the demeanor and procedures of working professionals.

Benefits for Employers

There are also benefits for employers that participate in a work-related program. They create a pool of skilled and motivated potential future employees. Those future employees tend to stay on the job. There are reduced training/recruitment costs as well as developmental opportunities for a current workforce. Some employers have used the student involvement to create new products or get involved in new projects. By participating in a program employers get to shape the curriculum. And of course, there is the benefit of providing a service to the community.

Benefits for the Schools

Schools also benefit from a work-related learning program. By addressing the needs of a diverse student population, they get to individualize their instruction for their students and make it relevant to them. Participating schools get to expand their course offerings and sometimes even their facilities. The faculty gets to interact with local businesses and both staff and students get the chance to work with state of the art equipment, technology and techniques.

Benefits for the Community

Clearly the community benefits from work-related programs too. The local economy is enhanced by students and employers working together and creating an environment of collaboration and cooperation among the school, the employers, and the community. Work-related learning can encourage respect, tolerance, and understanding among diverse groups within the community, fostering confidence in the school system as practical and beneficial results are observed.[9]

PRACTICE

The Kentucky Department of Education requires each school district in the state to submit a list of their career pathways prior to each school year. Included in the list are the proposed coursework and the criteria to identify how a student in each career major will be classified as career-ready.

In four of the ten Taylor County career pathways, the Kentucky Occupational Standard Skills Assessment (KOSSA) is administered to certify career readiness. In another, an industry certification is issued. In three others a capstone project or portfolio is submitted by the student for review. And in the other two pathways, successful completion of the coursework is required for the student to be identified as a completer.

High school principal Laura Benningfield says, "I believe that performance-based education (PBE) provides the perfect foundation for a strong career focus for the high school students. PBE allows students to move more freely at their own pace in core classes (and in many CTE courses). The students can not only major in a career pathway, but also take other courses related to their college/career interests or intern in a career-related field." The students at Taylor County High School are given a wide variety of career pathways. They include:

Agriculture

Teaching is a family affair for ag teacher Lindsay Wayne. Her father taught at TCHS and her brother teaches in the classroom next to hers. But it is her passion for teaching her students that is immediately obvious. "Going to class has never been at all appealing to me or any student, but Mrs. Wayne's class is something I look forward to. She makes it so we want to come to her class and learn," said one of her students in the online district newspaper.

Being a somewhat rural county, Taylor County Schools has a very strong and diverse agricultural program. In environmental science and natural resources systems students learn about plant and land science. They study forestry and horticulture, as well as wildlife and farm management. This course of study begins to prepare students for careers in forestry, horticulture, landscaping, and environmental resource management.

The horticulture program gives the students courses in greenhouse technology and floral design for those that are interested in greenhouse management and floriculture. Floriculture row crops provide some of the highest dollar per lineal foot yield of any cultivated crop today. Students can gain additional experience by working in the greenhouse, one of the student enterprises at Taylor County High School.

It is one thing to be able to grow crops or livestock, it is quite another to know how to profit from that skill. The agribusiness program, teaches everything from agricultural science to marketing and farm management. Small animal technology, equine science and veterinary medicine are all electives within this focus area.

No matter what you raise, you eventually use equipment. No matter how new the equipment is, it eventually must be repaired. And more than likely it must be repaired quickly. For those interested in agricultural mechanics, the program offers courses in small power equipment, agricultural power and machinery operations, and agricultural structures and design. And for those students interested specifically in animals, there are courses in animal science and animal technology.

Education

The career that Roger Cook wants all of his students to consider is teaching. He has been very successful in finding potential educators among his student body.

The early childhood concentration includes three sequential courses in early childhood services, as well as electives in relationships and nutritional science. The fundamentals of teaching concentration includes a course in early lifespan development and a course for dual credit on the principles of teaching. The early college program offers students the chance to take much of their freshman and sophomore coursework prior to graduation from high school. Because performance-based education is such a specialized discipline, TCS attempts to accommodate as many returning student teachers as possible.

Clint Graham is one of those students that returned. He teaches at the high school and coaches the girls' basketball team. His outlook and attitude are typical of the TCS staff. "I try to show them [the students and players] that succeeding in life is more important than succeeding in basketball. I try to prepare them for the future."

Culinary Arts

Cable television has given students exposure to the culinary arts. Students realize that food preparation can be big business. Many want to get a head start on a culinary education and are able to do so with this TCS program. The coursework includes nutritional science and sequential courses in culinary arts and is offered in a blended learning environment. Students gain additional cooking, preparation, and presentation experience through co-operative education opportunities and through participation in the Cardinal Corral, a student enterprise that caters many of the events at TCS. Three talented culinary arts students have qualified to compete in the Kentucky State Fair Cook-Off in 2015.

Business

Regardless of what business your career takes you into, you will need a working knowledge of finance. Students interested in finance take courses in accounting, financial services and computer applications. They can gain professional experience in this field by working in the bank at the high school, a student-operated financial enterprise supported by Citizens Bank and Trust. This institution manages savings accounts and personal loans for many of the students on campus.

The career pathway for those interested in marketing is particularly rich at TCS. The courses offered are in principles, retail marketing, and advertising/promotions. Available electives include courses in sports-event marketing and food marketing. Students can gain additional experience working for a local retailer through the co-operative education program, or by working at one of the student enterprises—a Kroger store in the high school and a specialty gift store.

The students that manage the grocery store received a call recently from the Kroger organization. The president of the company was going to be in the Campbellsville area and wondered if he could get a short presentation from the students. It happened that the teacher in charge of the program was attending a function in Atlanta. Without hesitation, the students told her it was not necessary for her to return, they would handle it. Two young men and two young women made the presentation.

The visitor was so impressed with their presentation, he asked one of the young men why he wasn't already working for Kroger. The student said that Kroger was not hiring when he needed part-time work, and so he got a job at the local Burger King. The student was told that if he wanted a job at Kroger, he could come back the next day. Laura Benningfield, the high school principal, believes it won't be long before that student will be a part of management at Kroger.

Businesses are always looking for high quality managers. Those students interested in a career in running and managing a business can take courses in fundamentals—accounting foundations, general business, and business management. Entrepreneurship and computer applications are offered as electives. As one of their cumulative projects, these students will be asked to design and plan their own retail operation. They will be expected to use their writing, presentation, and technology skills to complete and present the package.

A retail operation involves much more than just ringing up sales on the cash register. Students take the basic courses in principles, retail marketing and food marketing. They can choose computer applications, accounting, sports/events, promotions, advertising, or multi-media publishing as electives. These students can also work at local retail stores through the co-operative education program or by participating in the various student enterprises.

All marketing and retail students are encouraged to become members of DECA, an international students' organization that prepares emerging leaders and entrepreneurs in marketing, finance, hospitality and management in high schools and colleges around the globe.

Visual Art

Many students have an interest in pursuing the arts as a career. The creative arts are also part of the career pathways program at TCS. Started in the 2014–2015 school year, students interested in a career in fine arts select the visual arts pathway and begin with a basic art course and then progress to two-dimensional and three-dimensional courses. In place of passing a KOSSA or an external certification, students are required to submit a portfolio of their work to demonstrate their expertise.

Graphic Design

The graphic design pathway is for students interested in careers that involve electronic illustration. They study digital design, illustration, and photography. They gain additional professional experience by working on projects with the district marketing staff. An industry certification or a KOSSA certificate is required for them to demonstrate career readiness.

Instrumental/Vocal Music

For those students interested in a career in music, three sequential courses in band or chorus are required for career readiness in this pathway. A student must demonstrate mastery through a performance-based capstone portfolio to be certified for instrumental or choral music.

Performing Arts

This pathway for those students interested in acting, directing, or the technical aspects of drama production is new for the 2015–2016 school year. A series of courses in theater arts is necessary to be certified in this career. And again, a student must demonstrate proficiency through a performance-based capstone portfolio.

Engineering and Manufacturing

Tech design, principles of engineering and technology, and introduction to manufacturing are the required courses. A computer-aided drafting course in the fundamentals of engineering is an elective in this program. A capstone project demonstrating the student's proficiency is necessary to prove career readiness.

Allied Health

With the nation's demographics leaning toward a majority of older adults, the health and wellness field is one that will always be looking for qualified professionals. Not to mention the difficulty of finding and funding school nurses. The allied health career path features courses in pre-nursing and leads to an SRA industry certification. This program has been expanded recently to double the number of students to thirty. A blend of up-to-date technology and hands-on skill training are used to train students in this career path.

Aviation

This is not an "official" pathway, although the combination of flight simulators, technology, and avionics (airplane mechanics) makes this a very popular program. Students compete every year in a statewide competition to design a model airplane wing to maximize a certain aspect of aircraft design. This year it was lift, the year before it was cargo capacity. The team from Taylor County High School won the competition in 2014 and came in second in 2015.

Students in the program are able to log hours toward their certification because one of the part-time instructors at the school is a certified mechanic. Laura Benningfield remembers one student last year that simply didn't like the discipline of the academics at school. He began the aviation program and was hooked. He has now graduated and is enrolled in the avionics program at Somerset Community College. "Getting his certification at Somerset, he will be set for life," she said.

Benningfield says that when TCS originally proposed the aviation program to the state department of education for approval, they asked how many pilots did she think were needed in Campbellsville. She explained to the state educators that the program was not just a program for pilots, but prepared students for careers in aircraft design and aircraft mechanics as well and these were certainly fields in need of qualified professionals. The program is currently included under a "Transportation" career pathway.

Information Technology

This is a pathway that Benningfield wants to develop. With as much technology as the district has in place, it only makes sense to develop in-house talent in programming and coding as well as technology repair. Currently, she is looking for the right person to teach the program, but is philosophical about the difficulty of locating the right person. "I need a person that is talented in a variety of areas. If I can't find them, I won't offer the program this year."

Regional Vocational Program

The Green County Area Technology Center is a regional facility that provides courses in automotive technology, business technology, electrical technology, health science, machine tool technology, welding and wood manufacturing. TCS students taking courses at GCATC usually spend four of seven periods during the school day at the technology center. Vertical articulation to Elizabethtown Community and Technical College or Somerset Technical College is offered as well.

Expectations

By their junior year in high school, most students are expected to declare a career preference. By encouraging each student to sample a career pathway, Taylor County hopes to develop the soft skills necessary for each student to be successful and through project-based learning to develop the problem solvers that are in high demand in today's job markets.

NOTES

1. Threeton, Mark D. "The Carl D. Perkins Career and Technical Education (CTE) Act of 2006 and the Roles and Responsibilities of the CTE Teachers and Faculty Members." *Journal of Industrial Teacher Education*, 2007: 66–82.

2. Castellano, Marisa, James R. Stone III, Sam Stringfield, Elizabeth N. Farley-Ripple, Laura T. Overman, and Roshan Hussein. *Career-Based Compreshensive School Reform: Serving Disadvantaged Youth in Minority Communities*. St. Paul: National Research Center for Career and Technical Education, 2007.

3. Plank, Stephen. *Career and Technical Education in the Balance: an Analysis of High School Persistance, Academic Achievement and Post-Secondary Destinations*. St. Paul: National Research Center for Career and Technical Education, 2001.

4. Dewey, John. *Experience and Education*. New York: Collier Macmillan Publishers, 1938.

5. Clark, Robert W., Mark D. Threeton, and John C. Ewing. "The Potential of Experiential Learning Models and Practices in Career and Technical Education & Career and Technical Techer Education." *Journal of Career and Technical Education*, 2010.

6. "Effective Strategies for Dropout Prevention." National Dropout Prevention Center/Network. 2015. http://www.dropoutprevention.org/effective-strategies (accessed April 13, 2015).

7. Schargel, F. P., and J. Smink. "Strategies to help solve our school dropout problem." *Eye On Education*, 2001: 212.

8. Balfanz, Robert, John M. Bridgeland, Joanna Hornig Fox, Jennifer L. DePaol, Erin S. Ingram, and Mary Maushard. U.S. Department of Education, Office of Career, Technical and Adult Education Data. Washington: Civic Enterprises, et al., 2014.

9. North Carolina Department of Instruction. Benefits of Workplace Learning. 2015. http://www.dpi.state.nc.us/cte/curriculum/work-based/benefits/ (accessed April 13, 2015).

NINE
S.T.A.R.S.

The room is down in the basement of the largest elementary school in the State of Kentucky. It is very quiet even though there are seven high school students and seven elementary students working one-on-one on a literacy exercise. The high school students are members of a program called S. T. A. R. S.—Students Teaching And Reaching Students and have expressed an interest in teaching. The first- and second-grade students being tutored are students that for one reason (or many) are at risk of falling behind in reading and have been referred to the program by their teachers. The coach is a Reading Recovery specialist who instructs the tutors and sometimes the first- and second-graders.

THEORY

Roger Cook began the S.T.A.R.S. program six years ago. The original idea was to get the best and brightest students excited about the teaching profession, specifically about teaching in Taylor County. Hoping that the experience of teaching in an innovative and academically stimulating program like his, would make them seriously consider teaching as a career. Since no post-secondary programs taught performance based methodology, the teachers he hired needed extensive professional development—delivery, technology, organization, individualized education plans, etc. He was hoping to avoid at least some of that training by getting his students interested in teaching as a career and then hiring them as teachers once they finished college. Former students that know the culture and the methodology make great role models. It is the equivalent of re-investing the profits from a business.

Cook's idea to use his own alumnae as teachers reminded me of Geoffrey Canada's dream for Harlem Children's Zone (HCZ). Canada's idea was not only to make HCZ students successful college graduates, but also to interest many of them into returning to Harlem to teach and influence the next generation of students.

Cross-Age Tutoring

The influence of older children on the young is well documented. A child's older siblings influence everything from eating habits to social behavior. So why not use the influence of an older student to positively change academic outcomes? Using cross-age mentoring and tutoring, the at-risk students are not only more likely to want to perform better, but also to be interested in learning the skills that will help them perform better academically.

In a meta-analysis of fifty-five mentoring studies, DuBois, Holloway, Valentine, and Cooper[1] found that the most successful mentoring programs:

- •*monitored program implementation*—Cross-age tutoring and mentoring is much easier to consistently monitor if it is scheduled as part of the school day, but both during school and after school schedules come with some logistical problems that must be addressed prior to beginning the program.
- *provided ongoing training to mentors*—Mentors must be trained and that training should be included in the program.
- *involved parents,* Parents of mentors and mentees should be involved, since support at home makes the program all the more effective.
- *structured activities* for the mentors and mentees—Structured activities in the form of a basic lesson plan for academic activities and a plan for other activities that identifies goals to be accomplished.
- *clarified expectations* about frequency of meetings—This is particularly important if the program is scheduled after regular school hours.

DuBois et al. found that the presence of all five of these components doubled the effectiveness of mentoring programs. The Taylor County Schools' 1:1 S.T.A.R.S. tutoring program for first- and second-graders includes each of these elements.

Early identification and intervention for students at risk of falling behind is critical to maintaining high academic standards. While much is done to maintain and/or improve attendance for at-risk children by the Taylor County Schools Dropout Prevention Coordinator, improving attendance is often not enough to improve proficiency. Remediation is particularly important during the early years when basic skills are acquired and practiced. Teachers intervene through the Response to Intervention program and informally every day, but students also help other students.

In the S.T.A.R.S. 1:1 tutoring high school seniors mentor first- and second-graders to improve their reading skills.

If students are not on grade level in reading and math by third grade, they are at high risk of low academic performance or dropping out when they reach high school. Understanding that, in order to be truly effective a zero dropout policy must impact the students at every grade level, TCS uses cross-age tutoring to encourage academic progress for the six-and seven-year -old students.

If a child has difficulty reading, much of the material of the educational program is either lost or incomprehensible to them. The biggest challenge for educators is making sure that all children become competent readers. Those students who struggle in reading quickly fall behind their more skilled classmates. This gap in reading skills can emerge as early as first grade and, once present, tends to persist over time. First grade teachers can usually predict with uncanny accuracy, for example, those children in their classrooms with significant reading deficits at the end of the school year that will have continuing difficulties in reading, even in the fourth grade.

A major explanation for why poor readers lag so far behind typical readers in the same classroom appears to be simple lack of practice. Skilled readers tend to enjoy reading and to have lots of opportunities to use their reading skills independently. Poor readers, on the other hand, are likely to find reading to be difficult and frustrating. Not surprisingly, they avoid reading and therefore seldom practice to improve their literacy skills. The difference in ability between competent and less-able readers may be relatively minor in the early primary grades. However, good readers quickly sail far past poor readers, propelled by the momentum of continual reading practice.[2] While the long-term negative impact of poor readers can be enormous, the good news is that schools can train their own students to deliver effective tutoring in reading to beginning readers. Cross-age tutoring answers the nagging problem of delivering effective reading support to the many struggling young readers in our schools. Furthermore, peer-tutoring programs can improve the reading skills of tutors as well as tutees[3] and—in some studies—have been shown to build tutor's social interaction skills as well.[4] Young children tend to find the opportunity to read aloud to an older student to be reinforcing, adding a motivational component to this intervention.

Nationally the Big Brothers/Big Sisters program has substantial longitudinal data that indicates a student's relationship with a caring adult is critical to a student's success. The S.T.A.R.S. program uses the same patterns of influence and expectations as well as the social gravity of a one-on-one relationship with a young adult to connect the younger struggling readers to improved academic performance. What six- or seven-year-old can resist the exhortations, assistance, and praise of a seventeen-year old? This relationship connects both mentor and mentee to their school and to school academic activities. Cross-age mentoring in a student-centered environment is particularly fulfilling. The older students are there because they want to help. The younger students are there because they need and want the help. And once they form a connection with their mentor, they want to be there because they don't want to disappoint them. The same is true of the teenagers. I was told that one student came to tutor her mentee although she was not well. As soon as her tutoring session was over, she went to the school nurse. Her coach admired her dedication, but said she hoped all that passed between them was the day's lesson.

Teaching Assistants

Subject mastery is enhanced by many forms of practice. Teaching a subject and being able to explain the details is by far one of the most effective ways to achieve mastery. Giving students the opportunity to tutor other students, provides the chance to demonstrate and perfect their subject knowledge. These more able students not only provide role models for the others, but also move their protégés toward proficiency, and ultimately mastery. But this is not a one-way street. Although research has tended to focus on the outcomes for the mentees, there are also positive results for the high school mentors that come from coaching, mentoring, and acting as a role model for others. The emotional intelligence, maturity and personal discipline that are developed as a result of a cross-age or peer relationships are priceless. This kind of program gives mentors interested in a teaching career an opportunity to participate in an apprenticeship and there is an extremely high level of expectations for the S.T.A.R.S. students. Some will no doubt find that they are not cut out for teaching as a career, but others will find that they enjoy it and are excited about it. So the district derives benefits too. Many of these students that participate in the program have expressed a desire to make teaching a career. While Roger Cook was dining at a local restaurant recently, he was approached by a local college student. She introduced herself as a graduate of Taylor County High School and an education major at the university. She then asked to be given a practice teaching assignment at the high school. She knew what it would be like to teach in a district that supported performance-based education and she was eager to begin her career there. Like many performance-based education graduates, she wanted to come back and teach in the program that made her successful.

A study in *Health Education Research*[5] found that the presence of school-based natural mentoring relationships encouraged school attachment and a student's school attachment reduces risk behaviors. These results were statistically significant far beyond the potential influence of youth's age, gender, ethnicity, and household composition. School attachment, also referred to as engagement, is important because engaged students tend to be more successful students. Students that are engaged in their learning and attached to the school are more attentive and focused, they tend to use higher level critical thinking skills, and have more meaningful learning experiences. But how do we know that students are engaged? Roger Cook does his weekly teacher evaluations by watching the students, not by watching the teachers. He wants to see that the students are focused on learning, that they are alert and following the lesson and that they are taking notes or working on their electronic devices. They should be listening and participating in discussions about the lessons. They should be asking questions about the content of the lesson. They should be responding to questions. And he wants them to be animated and reacting to what is happening in the class.

Mastery, as Daniel Pink explains in his book, *Drive*,[6] is one of three elements that provide motivation for improving results on complex tasks. Although proficiency is celebrated, mastery is clearly the goal of every exercise in education, whether it is mastery of a specific topic or simply mastery of a group of facts. But it is clearly more than that. Mastery is the remarkable acquisition of a group of facts and skills that can then be applied in a wholly unrelated way to a problem that has never been discussed as part of a lesson. Subject matter mastery means that we understand concepts, not just rules of thumb or theorems. That application of a concept to a wholly unrelated problem is the goal of education. Sometimes termed critical thinking, it is the gold standard for the acquisition of knowledge. The teenagers involved in the S.T.A.R.S. program must problem solve every day. The students they are helping have not acquired the basic knowledge or skills on the first pass. It's now up to them to re-teach and make sure these students are prepared to succeed in the years ahead. This cannot be just a repetition of the lessons that went before. That didn't work. In the re-teach they must identify what is preventing the acquisition of this skill or knowledge and then explain it in a way that the mentee understands. The approach may be unusual, but it is not far from the guidance that Roger Cook imparts to his staff. "We have a problem? Let's figure out the best way to fix it."

Internships

There is a solid body of research to indicate that the internal and external internships that Roger Cook and Kelly Milburn are doing in Taylor County provide their students with the career-readiness skills so important for student success after graduation. Peter Parilla and Garry Hesser have said in their journal article in *Teaching Sociology* that experiential education promotes students' abilities to apply the sociological perspective to understand their lives.[7]

"The individual moves from being a passive consumer of information to becoming an active, aware, responsible citizen, focused not only on his/her own personal development, but also on becoming an agent of change . . . they are assuming meaningful roles and responding to real issues in ways that have long-lasting impacts on their own lives, as well as the lives of those whom they are serving"[8]

The internships and the corresponding responsibilities and personal interactions create an environment in which the students acquire and practice the skills they will need in their careers. Some researchers actually believe that the on the job learning teaches skills like critical thinking better than classroom activities providing "superior learning outcomes for service-learning as compared to classroom instruction for tasks requiring critical thinking and application of skills, while not detracting from fact acquisition learning."[9]

Subject mastery involves not only the acquisition of knowledge, but the ability to apply that knowledge to seemingly unrelated situations. Internships allow students to practice application of acquired skills and knowledge in a relatively low-risk environment.

PRACTICE

High school students apply for the program in March of their junior year. In the 2014–2015 school year, there were 189 S.T.A.R.S. at Taylor County High School. They participated in one of four programs. They were placed in 292 jobs inside and outside the school system. These students are the tutors, the teacher's assistants, the receptionists, and the technology repair technicians. They save the system thousands of dollars and gain priceless experience in the process. One of the programs involves internships in the community—communications at the local university, pediatric therapy for autistic children, or trail clearing in a state park. Another program involves work within the schools in everything from computer repair to sales. Another program lets students work as teachers' assistants. There are also S.T.A.R.S. taking an introductory college course in education and then working in their area of interest. And one of the more rigorous programs sends high school student to the elementary school for cross-age 1:1 tutoring of the first and second graders that are struggling with reading.

All three of Taylor County Schools are on the same seven period schedules. The elementary school is located roughly five minutes away from the secondary schools, which are currently on the same campus. Shuttle buses run during every class change between the elementary and the secondaries and between the secondaries and the elementary. This permits the S.T.A.R.S. to move easily between the schools and return to their next scheduled class.

1:1 Tutoring

When one of your rules is that no student is allowed to fail, you must use every tool in the toolbox to address the needs of the students that are at risk of falling behind. Students Teaching And Reaching Students is one of the tools.

The young participants are recommended by their first- and second-grade teachers based upon data and teacher observation. Students selected for peer tutoring should score in the 10–25 percent on MAP and should not be receiving additional reading assistance (RTI, ECE). Students should not have behavior plans. The ability to read, as discussed before, is one of the keys to progress. Students that lack that ability are coached using the reading recovery methodology by their high school mentors. The tutoring includes on-going training for the tutors in the essential elements of the process and the use of research-informed treatments to improve the reading skills of the first- and second-graders. The tutoring program supervisor conducts "tutoring integrity checks" and frequently monitors the reading progress of the first- and second-graders.

The tutoring program supervisor is very quick to tell interested students that they need not be perfect students to participate in the program. She says she would like high school students who have a desire to work with and help elementary students. They need to read comfortably at or above their grade level. They should be willing to accept a helping role in working with younger students. They should be students for whom school attendance is a priority. They should behave appropriately when working with younger children with limited adult supervision. And they should be able to be trusted when walking through the halls unaccompanied when picking up or dropping off the child to be tutored.

The continuous training in the tutoring program involves following a simple set of strategies and reliably assessing students using the AIMS Web, the Phonics Survey, the Dolch Word Lists, and the Slossan Word Test.

A typical lesson would involve word work on whiteboards, magnetic letters, and flash card review (five minutes), familiar rereading with model phrasing, expression, and fluency (five minutes), a guided lesson with introducing a new book and assisting tutee, as needed (fifteen minutes) and a journal write (five minutes), all components of Reading Recovery. The current program supervisor is a certified instructor in this methodology.

Just as any successful program in the school requires administrative support beyond the classroom, so does the S.T.A.R.S. tutoring program. The elementary principal gives verbal support to the program and its students. She assists the tutoring program supervisor by finding space and locating materials needed for tutoring. Like every good administrator, she works to eliminate roadblocks that threaten to interfere with peer tutoring. Just as importantly, she encourages staff and community support for the program.

The support and encouragement of the classroom teachers is also a key element of the program's success. They know that with few exceptions, peer-tutoring sessions should always be given priority in the student's classroom schedule. If the student does need to miss a tutoring session because of a classroom scheduling conflict, the teacher notifies the program supervisor in advance. They realize that peer tutoring is an important component of instructional support, not a privilege to be withheld as a consequence for student misbehavior. Although it is easy to view the program as a reward because the students enjoy it so much, students are never prevented from attending peer tutoring as a form of punishment and "Fun activities" like parties or playground are avoided during the tutoring time. Tutoring times are selected so that they do not interfere with activity or math times and are supplemental to regular classroom instruction in reading.

Of course, the S.T.A.R.S. program director is also critical to the tutoring program's success. She works closely with the supervisor. If necessary, she administers disciplinary action to tutors for lack of attendance, tardiness, attitude, etc. She assists with the selection of tutors and reviews the tutoring schedules to ensure continuity.

Without the peer tutoring program supervisor's expertise the program's success would be in jeopardy. Her work involves analyzing the data for student selection, locating an appropriate space in which to offer the program, training the high school students in the methodology, observing the tutoring sessions for quality control, and using curriculum based assessments to track the effectiveness of the program. She also assesses the elementary students using AIMS Web, models lesson components for the tutors, communicates student progress to teachers and administrators, designs individualized lesson plans, organizes tutor resources for easy access, and organizes and stores crucial information and data.

The elementary students participate in the tutoring sessions four days a week. The early release day still has seven shorter periods. During the period that they would normally tutor, the students plan lessons for the next week.

Local Internships

Placement in internships is directly related to what a student identifies as his or her interests on their application to the program. It is available to high school seniors. Kelly Milburn, the current program director, says she wants these students to acquire the soft skills necessary in their career—interviewing, dealing with people, wearing the appropriate attire, punctuality, reliability, etc. She also wants them to understand the value of service to the community and to the school. These are the important life lessons that she wants the students in the program to get.

The employer receives a packet of information outlining expectations. An informal follow-up occurs every two weeks and a formal observation occurs every nine weeks. Out placement to community employers is handled very carefully since it is in the program's best interest to maintain a continuing partnership with these local businesses. Almost all of the students placed have decided on careers in which they interned.

Last year, interns were placed in a pharmacy and a law office. The pharmacist said that many first-year pharmacy students that worked with him had never spent a full day behind the counter. Once they realized what the job was like, they dropped out. The Taylor County senior who interned at the pharmacy became certified as a pharmacy technician and has now gone to university with every intention of getting a graduate degree in pharmacy. The Taylor County senior that interned at the attorney's office prepared written case summaries and spent time in court with her employer assisting him by locating the pertinent summaries. She is headed to law school after her bachelor's degree.

The Campbellsville University Communications Department has three interns working with them learning the business. Two of these interns are helping the department write and edit internal and external communications—newspapers, newsletters, etc. Both are planning careers in writing. The third intern has been working in the video broadcasting field running cameras and taping and editing videos. He is very interested in a career in radio, and he will be transferring soon into that part of the communications department.

The Campbellsville Library has a Taylor County intern. She will likely enroll at Campbellsville University next year while continuing to work at the library, because "they don't want her to leave."

There is also one intern who expressed an interest in forestry. He has an internship at the local state park, clearing trails and doing site maintenance. All indications are that he will have a summer job at the park this year and a career as a forest ranger in the future.

Kid Spot, a local pediatric therapy organization, had an intern that worked with them last year helping with the activities related to therapies. This year they have an intern who prefers clerical duties and is working in the office. She might continue to do so after graduation because they too would like her to stay.

School Internships

S.T.A.R. Students at TCS are given internships within the school system. Again, these are jobs for which they have expressed an interest in their application process.

In a school district in which no one can drop out, every student absence is important. Students that assist in the front office call the homes of absent students every day to check on them. The students help with attendance records, phone calls, reception, and errands, and they substitute for the secretaries if they are absent.

Two students have asked to work as part of the custodial team at the high school. One of them helps clean up the cafeteria in the afternoon and another student helps clean the gym after school and after games. It is likely that they will be hired after they graduate.

Two students help with appointments and logistics in the guidance office. Recently, one of them was in the office when the counselor was out. A student came in and wanted to see the counselor, needing some comfort about the particularly bad day she was having. Having watched the counselor many times in the past, she was able to calm the student until the counselor returned—another example of the level of maturity that these students acquire through their time as interns.

Other student interns are placed into various positions in the student enterprises. Three students work on the tBAY site, the district's Internet auction site. Several students work in the gift shop that offers gift baskets for special occasions, monograms and embroidery, and school spirit merchandise. Two students operate the slushy machine ($1.00 after 3:00 pm). Several students work in the campus grocery store—a convenience for students and teachers who don't want to have to stop to shop on the way home or want to pick up something for lunch. Several students operate the campus bank, which opens at fourth period. That's just in time to get a loan, if you don't have money for lunch! One student works in the IT department. (He is the person that the staff calls when some device isn't working the way it should.) He also does all the video streaming for the sports teams.

A group of students run the Apple iPad program in the middle school and the Lenovo Yoga program at the high school. Devices are brought in for charging overnight or for repairs (they are Apple certified). Students begin loading the charged devices onto the teacher's carts at 6:00 am and unload the carts and place the devices in the chargers after school. This is an impressive and well-organized operation, so impressive that Apple sent six high level executives from Cupertino to check it out. The students run the middle school operation completely by themselves. Although everything is videotaped, there is no supervisor on site. If a teacher or any community member drops their phone or tablet and breaks the glass, the I Tech team can replace it quickly and economically.

S.T.A.R.S. as Teaching Assistants

As indicated earlier, Roger Cook wants his best and brightest students to get excited about teaching. That is why he began the program. He hopes that serving as teaching assistants will get them interested in teaching as a career. Much of this work is not just running copies or distributing papers. Although some students prefer to be assigned that work, many prefer more complex duties. The work that many are assigned is like the work a graduate assistant performs at the post-secondary level. Their work is supervised, but the students are given the opportunity to practice teaching and to serve as peer tutors in the classrooms. They are a part of the teaching staff for their assigned class. They go on field trips and attend all the other class activities.

An instructor from Campbellsville University teaches ED 102 Introduction to Education at the high school for interested students. That course covers the Kentucky teacher standards, licensing requirements, unit development, assessment development, classroom diversity, technology integration, and classroom discipline.

The majority of the S.T.A.R.S. are used as teaching assistants in the Pre-K through 3 classrooms. They work as typical teaching assistants, leading small group instruction and in general helping the teachers with their program delivery. These students are doing so much that if they are ever absent, the teacher needs a substitute. One teacher is paying her former S.T.A.R., now at the local university, to return and help her two days a week.

Two of the seniors are ESL students fluent in Spanish. They work with newly arrived students by translating, mentoring, and teaching language and reading skills. They function as student and parent advocates, putting both at ease in what can sometimes be stressful situations. There are two students that work with the special education students, assisting those teachers with all sorts of physical and occupational therapy activities and exercises.

In middle school, the student teaching assistants are used as tutors for math and science. The classrooms are flipped (lessons videotaped and available on the Internet), so the class work is more individual exercises. The assistants also help during science lab experiments. There are eight students who have expertise in the arts. They assist the art and music department with art projects, musical instrument training and dance choreography. The teaching assistants in the high school are tutoring calculus, statistics, AP history, math and science. There is one student who works as the science lab assistant. He prepares the materials for the experiments and then cleans the lab and stores the materials appropriately when the class is over. And two students assist the instructor in the two year award-winning aviation program.

Leadership

The director of the S.T.A.R.S. program at Taylor County Schools is a full time position. She started as part-time staff, but quickly realized that to be successful, the director needs to be a full time position. Milburn wants to expand the program to the local university by recruiting college S.T.A.R.S. She thinks they would be a great resource for a cyber-bullying prevention program. They also might be able to assist with the Stephen Covey programs that are already in the elementary (*Leader in Me*) and middle school (*Seven Habits of Effective Teams*).

NOTES

1. Dubois, e. a. (2002). "Effectiveness of Mentoring Programs for Youth: A Meta-Analytic Review." *American Journal of Community Psychology*, 157–97.

2. Stanovich, K. E. (1986). "Matthew Effects in Reading: Some Consequences of Individual Differences in the Acquisition of Literacy." *Reading Research Quarterly*, 360–406.

3. Ehly, S. (1986). *Peer Tutoring: A Guide for School Psychologists*. Washington: National Association of School Psychologists.

4. Garcia-Vazquez, E. (1995). "Best Practices in Facilitating Peer Tutoring Programs." In A. T. Grimes, *Best Practices in School Psychology*—III (pp. 403–11). Washington: National Association of School Psychologists.

5. Black, D., Grenard, J., Sussman, S., & Rohrbach, L. (2010). *The Influence of School-Based Natural Mentoring Relationships on School Attachment and Subsequent Adolescent Risk Behaviors*. Health Education Research, 892–902.

6. Pink, D. H. (2009). *Drive*. New York: Penguin Group Inc.

7. Parilla, P. F., & Hesser, G. W. (1998). "Internships and the Sociological Perspective: Applying Principles of Experiential Learning." *Teaching Sociology*, 310–29.

8. Mpofu, E. (2002). "Service-Learning Effects on the Achievement of Rehabilitation Services Students." *Michigan Journal of Community Service Learning*, 46–52.

9. Munter, J. (2002). "Linking Community and Classroom in Higher Education: Service Learning and Student Empowerment." *Journal of Nonprofit and Public Sector Marketing*, 15–164.

TEN

Student Ambassadors

> *"I have absolutely no doubt that among the students that are Taylor County's student ambassadors is a legislator or two. By the time they graduate, these individuals have the skills to be successful at whatever they want to do."*
> —*Troy Benningfield, former curriculum director for Taylor County Schools*

THEORY

Whether it is at the executive level of an organization or with the students in an educational institution, the identification of individuals with high potential within an organization is the first step for creating a leadership pipeline. The high potentials are given coaching and development opportunities that will ultimately lead to improving the organization.

Identification of High Potentials

In an article in the *Harvard Business Review,* Claudio Fernández-Aráoz and his co-authors say that the proper selection of high potential individuals is critical to developing a successful leadership pipeline. Designation of an individual as someone with high potential is complex. To reward someone with this designation is to identify them as an individual who possesses attributes to which others should aspire. If the selection process is flawed and the wrong person is rewarded, it is demoralizing and counter-productive.

The characteristics of a high potential fall into five categories according to the article: knowledge, skills, senior executive identity, leadership assets and motives. Clearly, knowledge and skills are the most obvious attributes and the easiest to improve. Senior executive identity involves a sense of self-identity. Do the candidates see themselves as leaders, not just for the prestige, but also for the opportunity to make things happen? Do they see themselves as helping other people?

Leadership assets consist of four elements. The high potential derives insight, engages others, demonstrates resolve, and seeks understanding. Motives are the last element and sometimes the most difficult to discover, but it is the most important. "The desire to have a positive impact on others for the good of the organization is a key predictor of executive potential."[1]

Cultivation of high potential student leadership is important for the health of the organization. High potentials are the core of an engaged student body. And an engaged student body is academically more successful.

In order to build engagement, Adam Gamoran and Martin Nystrand discuss the importance of taking students seriously, particularly in terms of the discourse between teachers and students.[2] Even though Gamoran and Nystrand are specifically talking about the level of instructional discourse (because the results are measurable), it stands to reason that the same is true of the interaction between teachers and students outside of class. Once a student understands that their opinions and ideas will be taken seriously, their level of engagement increases.

The students used as ambassadors have a responsibility to communicate that engagement to the organization's visitors. The skills they develop as student ambassadors serve them well both academically and socially.

Code Switch

Although the term "code switch" has historically meant the use of two languages within one's speech patterns in a single conversation, in 2013 National Public Radio (NPR) began a national conversation about race and culture that defined code switch more broadly. "Many of us subtly, reflexively change the way we express ourselves all the time. We're hopscotching between different cultural and linguistic spaces and different parts of our own identities—sometimes within a single interaction."[3]

The NPR conversation has been more about code switching between race and culture, but many of us code switch in this broader sense all the time. Our language and mannerisms change from our professional lives to our social lives and is dependent upon the person to whom we are speaking and our relationship to them. Some public figures have been embarrassed by the publicity of their Twitter tweets or their social media posts not matching their public persona. In other cases it is seen as simply being aware of your position and your surroundings.

"In January 2009, then-President-elect Obama went to Ben's Chili Bowl, a famous eatery in a historically black D.C. neighborhood. When the (black) cashier asks him if he needs change, Obama replies, 'nah, we straight.'"[4] It is awareness of the context and knowledge of the appropriateness of your patterns of speech and mannerisms that can help you become successful.

But how do students learn these "soft skills?" Students may code switch frequently as they interact with parents, relatives, teachers and classmates. The point is this: in order to be successful in school and in life, students must understand how to code switch and learn the contexts in which it is appropriate to do so.

Training in the Soft Skills

In the lectures accompanying his latest book, *Our Kids,* Robert Putnam emphasizes the acquisition of soft skills as a requirement for the social upward mobility of children.[5] He claims that soft skills (communication, critical thinking, logic, teamwork, etc.) are acquired at school through extra-curricular activities and advises the elimination of "pay-to-play" arrangements in school athletics for that reason. The Brookings Institution reports that in a recent national Pew Research Center study, adults were asked to pick from a list of ten skills which were most important for children to get ahead in the world today. Ninety percent of those surveyed said communication was most important. Teamwork was identified by 77 percent of those adults.

Brookings also analyzed the data from the 2010 Children of the National Longitudinal Survey on Youth (CNLSY) and concluded that there are "gaps in exposure to classroom activities related to building these important soft skills, particularly for low-income students."[6]

Taylor County Schools is far more deliberate than most about teaching these skills. Many of the programs available throughout the school day intentionally train students in the social skills they need to succeed. The student ambassadors program is one example.

PRACTICE

Student ambassadors at Taylor County Schools are taught social competence. They understand that communicating with visitors is different from communicating with their teachers. They understand that when Cook asks their opinion of a change in program he is considering, they can be candid but respectful. They know how to code switch their speech and mannerisms between lunch with their classmates and lunch with a visitor from another district. Speaking to a visiting state senator, they are more formal and perhaps somewhat less candid than they are when speaking to their friends.

This code-switch training is a feature of many of the programs at TCS. Students learn that their words, actions and even their attire should change based upon the situation. They are taught the appropriate attitude and vocabulary for job interviews and college applications. Whether it is the S.T.A.R.S., the student ambassadors, or the students in the career pathways program, they are mastering the soft skills. Although "code switch" is not part of the Taylor County Schools' instructional vocabulary, mastery of this very important set of skills is taught nonetheless.

History

The student ambassadors program has been in place at TCS since 2011. Troy Benningfield began the program when he became Instructional Supervisor at Taylor County Schools. Impressed with what he saw at Western Kentucky University (WKU) and their Spirit Masters, he thought creating a similar group at TCS would allow the steady stream of visitors to hear the student voice about the various innovations. The students conduct tours, create promotional videos, prepare brochures, and serve as Cook's student advisory council. He has since moved to Marion County (KY) Schools and has started a similar program there.

The history of the student ambassadors program at TCS starts to sound a little like the "begat" verses of the King James Bible. Troy Benningfield spent time at Western Kentucky University (WKU) attending seminars and workshops during his career as a teacher and was impressed with their student ambassador program which they call "Spirit Masters." WKU traces the origin of its program to a trip that Dr. Carl Kell, a professor of communication at WKU, made to the University of Alabama. While visiting, Dr. Kell met a group of student ambassadors and was impressed by these students. Dr. Kell suggested establishing a similar group to Western's Interim President, Dr. John Minton. (No doubt, Alabama's corps traces its origin to a similar faculty visit to another university.)

Ultimately, Dr. Kell and Nada McGuiness developed the student ambassador group known today as Spirit Masters at Western. The original group of students was selected in the spring of 1981. Twelve men and twelve women were selected and officially presented to the University that spring. The name of the group was taken from the University's motto: "The Spirit Makes the Master."

The Spirit Masters are the official ambassadors of Western Kentucky University. Through service to WKU, Spirit Masters are responsible for preserving traditions, striving for excellence, and making the Spirit of Western contagious. It is the role of Spirit Masters to not only promote WKU's spirit of hospitality to guests, but also inspire the student body to strive for the sense of excellence that WKU as a university reaches toward.

The selection of new Spirit Masters occurs in three parts: (1) Review of a written application with references, class schedule, unofficial academic transcript, and photo; (2) an initial interview of all applicants before a panel of three to four members of the University faculty, staff and administration; and (3) a final interview for selected applicants with the Spirit Masters Advisory Council and additional appointed individuals. WKU Spirit Masters are selected based on their performance in all levels of the selection process.[7]

The student ambassadors program at Taylor County began with 22 students. Similar to the WKU program, there is a written application process followed by an in-person interview. The student ambassadors program is available to students from elementary through high school.

The student ambassadors receive training during the summer in the skills required. They have visited Western Kentucky during some of the summer work sessions and met with the Spirit Masters. They role play everything from shaking hands to answering difficult questions in public. They are trained in public speaking and the appropriate manners for dining with guests. Students are given the chance to represent their school system and give visitors from all over the United States the student insights into the district's innovative programming.

Selection

While this is a very popular program at TCS, it is not a popularity contest. Students are selected for their potential, but not necessarily their ability to represent the school district on their first day as student ambassadors. Those students interested in journalism, communications, or hospitality industry careers are well represented in this program. Those students are particularly interested in the real world experience of meeting and greeting interested visitors and explaining performance-based education to them.

The extensive interview process includes evaluating students on attitude and potential. Although not a criteria, representatives from all socioeconomic segments of the community are selected. Susan Kilby, the assistant superintendent responsible for the overall program, says that selection day is particularly hard work.

The students are all assigned numbers when they apply with a teacher recommendation, since last names might influence the judges. In fact, judges were surprised one year to find that a principal's daughter was one of their inductees. The candidates socialize with both large and small groups and are evaluated. Their manners are observed at a luncheon. And, of course, they are interviewed one by one.

The group is comprised of student representatives from all district schools. The number of candidates selected depends upon the number of ambassadors that will be graduating. The corps stays at around twenty to twenty-five members. Once selected an ambassador serves until he or she graduates. Only one member, who after considerable coaching was still found unsuitable, was ever asked to leave. It is a prestigious program within Taylor County Schools and students that are not initially selected, often try again.

The Taylor County student ambassadors make special appearances at district events, provide campus tours, serve as the superintendent's advisory council, and promote good will throughout the school community. The responsibility for the program gives Susan Kilby a chance to connect with students. "It's one of my favorite things to do."

Equity

Although there are certain academic limitations for participation in a student ambassador program regarding grade point averages, the program provides an opportunity for students of all socioeconomic levels to demonstrate leadership as well as get training and life experience in skills that are certain to increase a student's likelihood of career success—public speaking and social interaction across various social strata.

"It is a real hardship for some of our parents, since they must get the students to school board meetings and other events that they would not otherwise attend. It is considered a real honor to have a student selected as an ambassador and they do it willingly," said Assistant Superintendent Susan Kilby.

She remembers one young lady who was selected in elementary school for her attitude, but not her presence or maturity. "It is amazing to see how far she has come." She is now a middle school student, and she recently spoke to and was interviewed by the Board of Education. (Those that act as greeters for the meeting are asked to speak to the board during the meeting.) Her poise and maturity were obvious as she answered questions and spoke to the board about her college and career plans.

Student Success

The ambassador program is one way TCS identifies students with high potential and grooms them for success in life. One former student ambassador is attending the University of Kentucky and has decided to become a pharmacist. Another former student ambassador is attending the University at Lexington; his major is education. The program creates high aspirations. Every former student ambassador has attended college.

Student Voices

Cook often asks these students for their opinions, asking them how to make a particular program attractive to students, or just asking them what's not working for them at school. They are not shy about sharing and he appreciates that. He genuinely wants to know what students think and what they want, and he gets that input unvarnished from the student ambassadors.

He asked for their input when he was beginning the Cardinal Academy. Because he listened that program is now over-subscribed. Their input will no doubt be used as the new schools are constructed and outfitted. Roger Cook believes they are an invaluable source of information. They function as a continuous focus group for him, making sure that his customers are getting what they need. They do not hesitate to "speak truth to power" and give him their opinions.

NOTES

1. Fernandez-Araoz, Claudio, Bors Groysberg, and Nitin Nohria. "How to Hang on to your High Potentials." *Harvard Business Review*, 2011.

2. Gamoran, Adam, and Martin Nystrand. "Taking Students Seriously." In *Student Engagement and Achievement in American Secondary Schools*, by Fred M. Mewmann, 40–61. New York: Teachers College Press, 1992.

3. Gene Demby. *Code Switch*. April 7, 2013. http://www.npr.org/blogs/codeswitch/2013/04/07/176352338/faq (accessed April 16, 2015).

4. Gene Demby. *Code Switch. Ibid.*

5. Putnam, Robert. *Our Kids: The American Dream in Crisis*. New York: Simon and Schuster, 2015.

6. Joanna Venator, Richard V. Reeves. "Building the Soft Skills for Success." Brookings. March 18, 2015. http://www.brookings.edu/blogs/social-mobility-memos/posts/2015/03/18-soft-skills-success-reeves (accessed May 19, 2015).

7. Western Kentucky Spirit Masters. 25 September, 2014. https://www.wku.edu/spiritmasters/ (accessed April 16, 2015).

ELEVEN
Response to Intervention

"A child mis-educated is a child lost." —*John Fitzgerald Kennedy*

THEORY

Response to Intervention (RTI), sometimes called Response to Instruction, combines assessments and interventions in a timely prevention system that is structured in multiple layers to maximize student achievement and/or reduce behavioral problems. With RTI, schools use reliable assessment data to identify students at risk for poor learning outcomes while frequently monitoring student progress. RTI provides evidence-based interventions and adjusts the intensity and nature of those interventions depending on a student's responsiveness. Ultimately, the program is also used to identify students with learning disabilities or other disabilities.[1]

RTI and Positive Behavior Intervention and Supports (PBIS) are now combined by some states and districts under a broader umbrella strategy termed Multi-Tiered System of Support (MMTS). MMTS features a wraparound structure of educational, community, and medical services to promote student success, but looks a lot like RTI as practiced in Taylor County Schools.

Many states include some form of RTI or MMTS in their descriptions of appropriate instructional methodology. Hughes and Dexter in their documentation for the RTI Network web site describe the elements necessary for a successful RTI program. They include:

- Extensive and ongoing professional development.
- Administrative support at the system and building level.

- Teacher buy-in and willingness to adjust their traditional instructional roles.
- Involvement of all school personnel.
- Adequate meeting time for coordination.[2]

Timing

One of the key components of RTI is the timing of the intervention. This is not re-teaching in response to a student's failing an end-of-course exam. RTI is remediation that takes place immediately upon identification of an issue. Like a medical diagnosis and a prescriptive cure, the timing of the assessment and the timing of the remediation are crucial here. The point of RTI is to avoid long-term negative learning outcomes by providing targeted teaching before the student falls behind.

RTI involves three levels of high quality preventions. The first step is the core instruction that meets the needs of most students that require remediation. The second prevention step is a series of evidence-based interventions of higher intensity in small groups for those at-risk students that have learning or behavioral challenges. The third step is a more intense (longer and more frequent) individualized intervention for students who have been through the second step and still have learning or behavioral issues.

Screening

In traditional RTI students are screened at the beginning of each school year in a two-stage process. The initial screening is a universal norm-referenced screening based upon a cut score and usually identifies those students that are potentially at risk. The second stage screening involves more in-depth testing to identify the student's specific issues and their at-risk status.[3]

Data

In her article in *The School Administrator*, Judy Elliott describes Response to Intervention as the practice of providing high-quality instruction and intervention tuned to students' needs, through frequent monitoring of student progress and the adjustment of instructional delivery based upon applying student-response data. She says that RTI "requires the knowledge, appreciation and continual use of data in making instructional and programmatic changes that are second nature to all consumers in the system—administrators, teachers, parents and the community."[4] NCRTI also mentions the use of reliable data to differentiate the remedial response.[5]

Data analysis and decision making are central to all three levels of RTI implementation. Teachers and administrators use screening and progress-monitoring data to make decisions about instruction and movement within the multi-level prevention system. "Once people see that data are a tool to provide tailored interventions for students and support for classroom instruction, trust is built, collegial relationships are forged and the realization emerges that we are in this for the betterment of all students."[6]

Benefits

The chief benefits of the RTI approach is the timeliness of the intervention, the use of assessment data to structure the delivery of the educational program, and the use of multiple levels of intervention tailored to the needs of the student.

The National Association of School Psychologists had these observations:

- RTI is an initiative for all education, cutting across general, compensatory, and special education. It can create a well-integrated and seamless system of instruction and intervention guided by child-outcome data from frequent progress monitoring.
- In RTI, research-based instruction and intervention are administered by qualified personnel, implemented with fidelity and integrity, and adjusted to address the student's individual difficulties.
- RTI is not owned by any one profession. Successful models are an authentic collaboration between administrators, educators, related services personnel, and parents.
- RTI provides opportunities for all team members to expand their traditional roles and responsibilities, to engage in a variety of service delivery options, and to take on new leadership opportunities, requiring a systemic change in the allocation of resources when conceptualizing personnel workloads.
- There is no "one size fits all" model for RTI. The federal government purposely provided few details for the development and implementation of RTI procedures, stating specifically that states and local districts should be given the flexibility to design models that reflect their unique situation.
- RTI involves less psychometric standardized approaches and more pragmatic, educationally relevant models focused on measured changes in individual performance over time.
- Involving parents and engaging them in a collaborative manner is critical to the success of RTI. Informed and involved parents are better equipped to support and reinforce academic and behavioral interventions at home.

- RTI approaches show promise for closing the achievement gap and for reducing disproportionality in special education for all student groups."[7]

Why RTI?

In their article in *School Leadership* Austin Buffum, Mike Mattos and Chris Weber say that the answer as to why to use RTI comes down to why educators have joined the profession in the first place—that is to help children be successful. "RTI should not be a program to raise student test scores, but rather a process to realize students' hopes and dreams. It should not be a way to meet state mandates, but a means to serve humanity. Once we understand the urgency of our work and embrace this noble cause as our fundamental purpose, how could we possibly allow any student to fail?"[8]

PRACTICE

From the literature one can get the impression that Response to Intervention is a highly regimented and prescriptive technique of remedial instruction. And while all the steps and all the terminology is there, in the hands of Roger Cook's creative professionals at Taylor County Schools, this program delivers instructional help to students that is highly personalized and attuned to a student's specific requirements.

The systematic evaluation of students and their abilities and the adjustment of instructional delivery to advance those students seems like just common sense to the educational staff at Taylor County Schools. Their RTI program has been designated by the Kentucky Department of Education (KDE) as the model for the state. In May of 2015 KDE is producing a webcast highlighting the program.

The marriage of performance-based education and RTI is a perfect match. The idea of "waiting to fail" that has characterized education in the past has no place in a protocol that creates a variety of instructional delivery methods and tries to place students in the best environment for them to learn.

Dr. Stephanie Wilkerson is a nine-year veteran of TCS and the district staff member responsible for their implementation of RTI. She says she cannot recall a time that she has asked the superintendent for something for a child in need that he has not taken care of it. Sometimes it has come out of his own pocket, when the district couldn't afford it. "We are not a district that has a lot of money, but somehow we seem to be able to do whatever it takes if it's going to make a difference to kids."

Purpose

While some teachers may see RTI as a way to get struggling students out of their classroom and into an alternative assignment, the teachers at Taylor County use RTI to make sure their students are properly placed. The same system that identifies students that need additional help is also used to accelerate those students who demonstrate their knowledge and ability to apply it on the assessments.

The universal assessments are used as initial indicators of proper placement. If a student can demonstrate that they have mastered the content, they are put into the next level. If a student cannot show understanding of the content, a second assessment is administered and discussions with the teacher are initiated. Help is given in the form of RTI Tier II (small group instruction). If progress monitoring indicates additional help is required, one-on-one intensive assistance is provided (RTI Tier III).

Only after these interventions have failed is a special education referral considered, and it is specific to the issue that is causing the student to struggle. "We have students that are in special ed for reading, but are accelerated in math," says Dr. Wilkerson. Like every other placement at TCS, special education is a differentiated assignment.

Logistics

The Measures of Academic Progress are used for the initial screening. They are given to students every six to eight weeks. Students' normative cut scores are used to identify students at the top and bottom. A student that scores above the ninetieth percentile is considered for acceleration (usually to the next grade level). A student that scores below the tenth percentile is considered for additional evaluation. AIMSweb and other tools are used for further evaluation. The student's progress is also discussed with his or her teacher for the additional source of information.

A team consisting of an intervention specialist, the school pricipal, the student's teacher, and Dr. Wilkerson meet and discuss the student's placement and what interventions are appropriate. A student's parents are often included as well.

Once a student is placed in Tier II or Tier III for interventions, an intervention specialist is assigned and student progress is monitored on a weekly basis. At any one time about 5 percent of the elementary school students are identified as being in need of intervention. There are six intervention specialists at the elementary school. There is one intervention specialist at the middle school and one at the high school. One measure of success is that there are far less students identified at the middle and high school levels, although the assessments are no less frequent.

Tier II services are given to students as small group instruction, normally five students or less. The evidence-based interventions are specific to the issues for which the students need help—phonics, reading comprehension, etc. The interventions are administered by trained student tutors (S.T.A.R.S.), or classified/certified personnel.

Tier III interventions are given to students as one-to-one or in some cases one-to-two tutoring. These sessions are done for a minimum of 30 minutes per day. If there is no evidence of progress after eight weeks in Tier III, a special education referral is considered.

Once a student's progress is measured at the 20th percentile, they are returned to their classes. The momentum of improvement often carries the student beyond just a return to their regular class. Many RTI students eventually move beyond their grade level and into accelerated classes.

Transfers

One unusual source of students not performing on grade level are transfer students from other districts. Dr. Wilkerson estimates there are "a handful of students" each semester that register at Taylor County Schools that have been unsuccessful at larger school districts. Some of these students come from dysfunctional families; some have just never taken an interest in school. Many come to TCS with few credits toward graduation.

These students and parents are often surprised at the flexibility of the programs and staff at Taylor County. One of the questions that Wilkerson usually asks is, "What do you want us to do to help you graduate?" She says students and parents often have better ideas than the staff specifically about how to get the student through school and back on track. Innovative programming to address every student's need is a hallmark of the district.

Cook's Rules

Remember that Roger Cook has three rules: (1) No child fails. (2) No student is held back because of their chronological age. (3) No dropouts. It would seem that these rules would apply an inordinate amount of pressure on the staff whose job it is to provide academic support to the students that are failing. Not so, said Dr. Wilkerson. She thinks the three rules are a result of a culture that is focused on students and that is about doing what is right for them.

When he began at TCS, he was very clear about what was expected and everyone that did not agree, sought employment elsewhere. The old system of tracking based upon intelligence, bad test scores, discrepancy models, and struggling kids being referred wholesale to special education didn't work. The Response to Intervention model he proposed to use made sense to Stephanie Wilkerson and her staff, and they have demonstrated that it can be effective.

NOTES

1. Essential Components of RTI—A Closer Look at Response to Intervention. Washington: National Center for Response to Intervention, 2010.

2. Hughes, Charles, and Douglas Dexter. "Field Studies of RTI Programs, Revised." *RTI Action Network*. n.d. http://www.rtinetwork.org/learn/research/field-studies-rti-programs (accessed April 22, 2015).

3. Essential Components of RTI—A Closer Look at Response to Intervention. *Ibid.*

4. Elliott, Judy. "Response to Intervention: What and Why?" *The School Adminstrator*, 2008.

5. Essential Components of RTI—A Closer Look at Response to Intervention. *Ibid.*

6. Essential Components of RTI—A Closer Look at Response to Intervention. *Ibid.*

7. "New Roles in Response to Intervention: Creating Success for Schools and Children." *NASP Advocacy*. 2007. http://www.nasponline.org/advocacy/rtifactsheets.aspx (accessed April 23, 2015).

8. Buffum, Austin, Mike Mattos, and Chris Weber. "The Why Behind RTI." *Educational Leadership*, 2010: 10–16.

TWELVE
Innovative Staffing

"Think about your work not in terms of what you do, but in terms of the role you play. Your role is not just your title, but includes sets of behaviors, tools, and approaches to create value for and with your organization." —Nilofer Merchant[1]

THEORY

There are many aspects to an innovative staffing strategy. The most obvious is how position descriptions are written and how deep or flat the hierarchy is within the administration.

A Great Place to Work

W. L. Gore & Associates is a company that researches, develops, and manufactures fluoropolymer-based products. One called Gore-Tex that is a lightweight, water-repellent fabric used in everything from jackets to footwear. Headquartered in Newark Delaware, the company employs over 9,000 people in 30 countries. Gore has made the *Fortune* magazine's annual list of "100 Best Companies to Work For" every year for the past sixteen years.

Founded by Bill and Vieve Gore in 1958, the company believes that job titles and organizational structures get in the way of innovation and creativity. So, every employee has the same title and job description—associate. Leaders in the organization are defined as someone who has followers and sponsors (not managers) are responsible for guiding your career.

Hiring at Gore is based upon attitude, and not simply qualifications. Team-oriented individuals who are self-actualized are most likely to be hired. Those that are just ambitious are not. Groups of associates are used to evaluate candidates. Once hired, an associate is expected to spend some time with various teams within the organization, find something of interest on which to work, and join a group of associates to pursue that work.

There are no more than 200 associates in one building. Buildings are located close to one another so that they can share services, but Gore believes that business benefits from the personal connections and informal communications that come from keeping things small.

Communications are open, direct, and two-way. If an associate has a question, they are encouraged to ask the person most likely to have the answer. All associates answer their own phones and leave their office doors open.

Associates are encouraged to select the projects they want to work on and the teams they want to work with. As long as there is a need for their skills and passion, Gore associates have the freedom and the responsibility to increase their contributions while building their expertise. Associates are expected to be as innovative with their career path as they are in their work.[2]

The Idea Factory

Hiring and developing highly talented staff is only one aspect of creating a great organization. The organization must have a culture that nurtures that talent and an environment that enhances their ability to use that talent. In his book describing the innovations at Bell Labs, Jon Gertner tells the story of the organization that gave us much of the technology we take for granted today. Not only was Bell Labs a resource-rich environment, but also it was an organization with high expectations and a loose hierarchy.

As Gertner explains, these young scientists were encouraged to "look beyond the day-to-day concerns that shaped the world of their fellow engineers . . . and focus on how fundamental questions of physics or chemistry might someday affect communications."

Bell Labs became the workplace of choice for many of the scientific luminaries of the time. Loosely organized into teams that were working on projects, the membership of those teams fluctuated depending on the issue at hand. And other senior researchers might be consulted, if their particular expertise was needed.

In 1916 Frank Jewett was put in charge of the engineering division of Western Electric. Inside the engineering division was a small group of scientists and engineers that was responsible for research. That group was under the direction of Harold Arnold. Jewett and Arnold were the men who found a way to transmit a transcontinental phone call from Alexander Graham Bell in New York to his old assistant Thomas Watson in San Francisco at the Panama-Pacific International Exposition in 1915. Bell Telephone at the time had about two million customers, mostly in the Northeast.

Although a few large German organizations had been successful in creating small research divisions in the past, no corporation had ever created a research laboratory on the scale of what was ultimately to become Bell Telephone Laboratories in 1925 under Jewett. Literally thousands of technical experts were employed in product development for the telephone business and roughly 300 worked on basic and applied research under Arnold.

The technical experts were free to pursue their own interests. The ultimate connection to communications was sometimes a very thin one. The culture was laid back and forgiving. The hours were not regular, the projects tended to be self-imposed, and the activities bizarre. Claude Shannon, a Noble Prize winning mathematician, electronic engineer, and cryptographer, often traveled the long hallways at the labs riding a unicycle and juggling.

Although the organizational structure appeared chaotic, Bell Labs technical experts invented satellite communications, the transistor, the microchip, the cell phone, microwave communications, information theory (how to communicate using Bollean algebra), not to mention all sorts of advances in telephony from dial tones to signal separators. This was an idea factory unlike anything before or since.[3]

Google

No description of innovative staffing would be complete without a mention of Google. In her book on organizational leadership, Amy Lyman describes it this way. "Google has created great power in their culture—the power that comes when you promote understanding, enhance participation, and extend influence through the sharing of information."[4]

Much has been written about the physical work environment for the staff at Google as well as the former policy of spending 20 percent of staff time on a creative project of choice. Less has been written about the specifics of Google's management strategy. This is an organization, much like Bell Labs, created by engineers for engineers. Also like Bell Labs, its future revenue stream is dependent upon innovation.

In the December 2013 issue of *Harvard Business Review,* David Garvin wrote an article about management at the organization. It seems even management in a company with a hierarchy as flat as Google's is a source of serious discussion. In fact Garvin says that founders Brinn and Page actually experimented with a structure that had no managers at all, but quickly revised that strategy because they were being bombarded with "questions about expense reports, interpersonal issues and other nitty-gritty issues."

Managers are still scarce in the company of over 37,000 employees—only 6,100 supervisory staff, with most managers responsible for more than thirty direct reports, thereby eliminating any tendency to micromanage.

"So here's the challenge Google faced: If your highly skilled, hand-picked hires don't value management, how can you run the place effectively? How do you turn doubters into believers, persuading them to spend time managing others? As it turns out, by applying the same analytical rigor and tools that you used to hire them in the first place—and that they set such store by in their own work. You use data to test your assumptions about management's merits and then make your case," writes Garvin.

After substantial Google research, Project Oxygen, the data intensive product of years of study of manager effectiveness, identified eight key behaviors of great managers. Since its initial rollout in 2010, Oxygen has been improved to include an awards program and a series of in-house training courses, one series for new managers and one series for senior staff.

Two evaluation instruments are used for staff to give their managers constructive feedback. An upward feedback survey (UFS) was created for employees in administrative and global business functions and a tech managers survey (TMS) was created for the engineers. Low scores are taken very seriously with low scoring managers often improving the most in the next round. It is no surprise that management at Google is supported by an innovative and data-rich staffing strategy. In fact, it is what you would expect of the company intent upon managing all of the information in the world.

"That, in a nutshell, is the principle at the heart of Google's approach: deploying disciplined data collection and rigorous analysis—the tools of science—to uncover deeper insights into the art and craft of management."[5]

PRACTICE

Taylor County Schools has a cadre of positions that are part of an innovative staffing strategy that are not typical of most school districts. The roles and responsibilities of these positions are created specifically to support performance-based education as practiced at Taylor County Schools.

Marketing Directors

Take for example, the marketing directors. Tori Gatewood and Maddie Gumm are in charge of selling TCS. The biggest event that the marketing directors orchestrate is the academic pep rally. The pep rally is an event held just before end-of-year testing to celebrate all of the hard work the students have done. Gatewood and Gumm secure over 10,000 dollars' worth of donations from the community. These prizes are raffled off to students during the pep rally with the biggest single prize being a car given to a deserving high school senior.

For the past two years the car has been donated by a local car dealer. Previously, Cook has purchased automobiles at a reduced price from the Drug Enforcement Agency or state law enforcement. These were not new cars, but after a repaint and repair from the district vehicle maintenance department, they were reliable transportation.

The gifts and donations that the marketing directors arrange to get from local businesses, organizations, and individuals range from technology to school supplies. The pep rally is an event that students and staff look forward to every year. The gym at the high school is packed with students from third grade to high school seniors. The staff is grinning and wondering what sort of entrance Roger Cook will make this year. (Last year he rode into the gym on his Harley.)

The prizes are given away by drawing the names out of a box. Students' names are put into the box based upon their academic record. For every time a student gets a proficient or distinguished assessment score, they get to put their name into the prize drawing—five times for distinguished (ninetieth percentile and above) and four times for proficient (seventieth to eighty-ninth percentile).

These become incentives for student performance, but because they are a random reward for performance, a chance to win a prize either large or small, they avoid the ineffective pay for performance gambit. The student that has barely made proficient on one test might win the biggest prize. The student that has made distinguished on all of their tests has a better chance, but still may not win a prize.

The marketing directors also orchestrate the Taylor County Schools' online auction site called tBay. Like eBay the site allows the district and the entire community to auction surplus or unneeded items. When an item is sold for a community member, 25 percent of the purchase price is kept by the district as a commission. The online auction has become a revenue generator for the district.

Gumm and Gatewood partner with local organizations for sponsorships. The TCS web site currently advertises nine local sponsors and a request for additional corporate sponsors is prominently displayed. They also sell naming rights for their buildings, fields, and stadiums and are responsible for sales brochures and social media for TCS.

Technology Integration Specialists

If teachers are to take advantage of technology in their classrooms, they need expert advice about available applications, presentation techniques, and development of online content. The technology integration specialists are on call to help with these issues. Originally locally funded positions, these are currently funded through the Race to the Top program, a federal funding stream that will end in 2017. This means that they serve all of the thirty-five school districts in the Green River Regional Educational Cooperative. As technology becomes more pervasive they will be able to spend less and less time helping Taylor County.

DiAnne Harris, Curriculum Coordinator for Taylor County, says that the positions are so valuable that when the grant funding is exhausted, TCS will have to find a way to fund them again. In fact, the ultimate plan would be to have a technology specialist at each school.

Jessica McCubbin and Sarah Hayes, the current technology specialists are both former classroom teachers. Passionate advocates for performance-based education and self-paced learning, they are both examples of how professional development is distributed within the district. They are on call to help teachers with whatever technology issues are in the way.

One interesting discovery they have made: in TCS flipping classrooms (i.e. virtual content at home and "homework" during class) was far less effective if the content was delivered by someone the students did not know. Their own teacher's presence on the content video meant they paid more attention and replayed what they didn't understand more often.

Virtual Program Teachers

The Virtual Academy has a full-time staff of certified and classified educators. As described in chapter 4 these individuals are both instructional and administrative. In addition to the usual educational problems, they are prepared to solve logistical problems as well. There are also content-area teachers that are scheduled as instructional resource into the Virtual Academy for one or two periods at a time as part of their teaching load. They are still given one period a day as a planning period, but instead of being scheduled to teach in a classroom, they are scheduled to be in the Virtual Academy as resource teachers.

This helps Jennifer Fitzpatrick, who is in charge of the lab. "I know a little bit about a lot of things, but certainly do not know everything. Having a subject matter expert in the lab for the students who have questions is crucial, so that the students can continue to move forward with their lessons."

College and Career Readiness Specialist

The educational accountability environment has meant that every district must be ready to report how many of their students are prepared for college or careers. Christy Parks, a certified guidance counselor, monitors each high school senior for college and career readiness.

College readiness in the State of Kentucky is assessed by students taking the American College Test (ACT). If a student doesn't pass the ACT, Parks administers the Compass Learning high school acceleration software. A student's successful completion of this regimen is used as an alternative indication of college readiness.

Career readiness in some pathways is measured in the State of Kentucky through the Kentucky Occupational Standard Skills Assessment (KOSSA). But KOSSA is not the only way to demonstrate readiness. In some pathways the student must qualify for an industry certification. In others, the student is required to produce a capstone project or submit a capstone portfolio for evaluation. Other courses of study require satisfactory completion of the coursework.

As the college and career readiness specialist, Parks attends to all of this and more. For those considering the military or curious about a career, the Armed Forces Vocational Aptitude Battery is an option. She has created job fairs and college fairs, a career day for middle school students, job shadowing programs, internships, and a certificate program in work ethics and skills.

The college and career readiness position at TCS is currently grant funded. The position is so valuable that local funding might have to be found, if grant funding is no longer available.

Dropout Prevention Specialist

Unlike a dropout prevention specialist in a typical school district, there is likely more pressure on this position at Taylor County Schools because the TCS board of education maintains a zero dropout policy. Karen Hayes, the dropout prevention specialist has a caseload of about 115 students. Her caseload runs the gamut from students that have transferred from other districts and are behind on their credits to graduate to TCS students that have spent two weeks in the juvenile detention center (in an adjacent county) and now need to catch up.

Her work involves one-on-one counseling and regular check-ins with struggling students. Struggling students are referred to the dropout prevention specialist by the guidance counselors. Cook is the court of last resort. He always says, "If you can't do anything with them, send them to me. If I can't convince them to stay in school, I will get a judge to order them to stay." And he has done so in a few cases.

Response to Intervention Teachers

The last group of individuals that Roger Cook credits with making performance-based education a reality is the group of successful teachers that work with the RTI intervention teams. As described in chapter 11, Response to Intervention is a rigorous multi-layered remedial effort that identifies students testing at ten percentile and below and helps them get to above the twentieth percentile and ultimately back on grade level. There is always a close working relationship between the RTI specialists and the students' teachers. As part of that effort, the most successful teachers are sometimes asked to teach a remedial class or help with a step in the interventions.

The Future

Roger Cook and his district rarely stand still. There are likely other positions, hybrid job descriptions, or other innovative programs that are being created as this is being written. Like the leadership of the companies mentioned earlier in this chapter, Cook realizes that in order for disruptive innovation to flourish in education, he must have an administrative structure that wholeheartedly supports it. Creative staffing and assignment of responsibilities is a critical component of this effort.

NOTES

1. Merchant, Nilofer. *The New How*. Sebastapol: O'Reilly Media, Inc., 2010.
2. Burchell, Michael, and Jennifer Robin. *The Great Workplace*. San Francisco: Josey-Bass, 2011.
3. Gertner, Jon. *The Idea Factory*. New York: Penguin Group Inc., 2012.
4. Lyman, Amy. *The Trustworthy Leader*. San Francisco: Jossey-Bass, 2012.
5. Garvin, David A. "How Google Sold Its Engineers on Management." *Harvard Business Review*, 2013.

THIRTEEN
Continuous Validation

> *It is the end of the school year celebration for Taylor County Schools' staff. Roger Cook always tries to do something unexpected. This year there is a $200 check taped under every seat. He says, "I wish I could give them more, but I'm not exactly Bill Gates. I think everyone knows I appreciate all the work they do for our kids."*

THEORY

Continuous validation is one way to motivate students and teachers to improve outcomes. There are several ways to provide that validation. Social rewards such as praise are one option, while tangible rewards (money, prizes, etc.) are another. But all forms of support come with collateral issues.

Praise

Even the way students are given praise for their work can affect their outcomes and their ability to bounce back from an initial lack of success. If they are praised for the process used or the difficulty of the work and not their intelligence, then students begin to view intelligence as a work in progress and not something you either possess or lack.

Dr. Carol Dwyer of the Educational Testing Service says that "process praise" can be constructive because it focuses the student on effort and work strategies when they are successful, rather than "person praise" which tells them they were successful because they were smart. This directly affects a student's approach to a problem, their attitude when they encounter initial failure, and ultimately whether or not they achieve.[1]

Dr. Dwyer finds that students whose teachers praise effort rather than intelligence will apply more effort when the work becomes difficult, they will seek challenges, and they will set higher goals for themselves. They tend to look at failures as opportunities to learn and increase their efforts. Ultimately they will learn more. "These findings are also related to achievement gaps. Students drop out of challenging programs or do not hold appropriately high educational aspirations for themselves because they believe or fear that they 'don't have what it takes' to succeed. In fact, the problem may be that these students need only to apply more effort or use different strategies in order to succeed."[2]

It turns out that the effect is even present in very young children. Research indicates that one- to three-year-olds if praised for ability rather than effort, tend to become more cautious and will avoid challenges. When a problem is difficult, they will withdraw, feeling they don't have the ability with which to solve it. Longitudinal studies have shown that this effect lasted for at least five years.[3]

Descriptive praise ("Providing the context for the problem was a good way to begin describing how you solved the problem.") is more effective than general praise ("Good job!"). If a student is given descriptive praise, they are told specifics about what they did successfully, and they are given some information about standards. However, the standards must be reasonable. If they are too high, children may become discouraged.[4]

But is praise really all that powerful? Social rewards (praise) and tangible rewards (money) can actually activate the same areas of the brain.[5] Clearly, this is something to consider carefully when making decisions about how to motivate students and staff.

Motivation 3.0

Daniel H. Pink believes we require an "upgrade" to the motivational operating system that runs behind most of our economic and social interactions.[6] He believes we think about motivation incorrectly and cites research that indicates performance on complex tasks is not enhanced through rewards. Alfie Kohn made the same point about education in his book, *Punished by Rewards*.[7]

Pink reminds us that Motivation 2.0 (that's the if-then reward system) only works on routine tasks, and then only because the task itself requires very little, if any, intrinsic (internal) motivation. Therefore, the extrinsic reward does not interfere with what is required to get the job done. If the work to be done is creative, right-brain work, "you're on shaky ground offering 'if-then' rewards. You're better off using 'now-that' rewards. And you're best off if your 'now-that' rewards provide praise, feedback and useful information."[8]

In Pink's Motivation 3.0 construct, a now-that reward is given after a task is completed successfully. It is a virtually random occurrence, and therefore not expected. It is not usually the same reward twice in a row. Even a "Thank you" or an "I appreciate what you do" becomes devalued over time, if used for every completed project large and small regardless of the quality of the work or the effort involved.

Connection and Empathy

Continuous validation of staff and students becomes a delicate balance. It is nonetheless a method of reinforcing personal connections. Author and researcher, Dr. Brené Brown, is the expert when it comes to analyzing and describing connections—what works and what gets in the way. "Connection is why we're here; it is what gives purpose and meaning to our lives."[9]

In exploring connections, Brown delves deep into her research on empathy. Empathy is the capacity to acknowledge our own experiential lens and have the ability to put it aside and see someone else's perspective. She says the less privileged among us tend to be taught this from birth. Those of privilege in many cases must be taught this skill as it has not been part of their upbringing. Empathy is a shame inoculant and is the doorway to helping a student toward shame resilience.

How is this related to learning? Because the K–12 continuum is a learning experience for children and young adults, shame is an integral part of the package. "I'm just too dumb to get this." Or "Why am I such an idiot?" Or "I'm just not good at . . ." All of these are shame indicators. If we are able to provide empathy (i.e. connection without judgement) in these situations, we can move students toward learning.[10]

PRACTICE

Taylor County Schools celebrates their students and their staff. There is a celebration for students and a celebration for staff. Roger Cook tries to deliver the unexpected at both gatherings.

The Roger Awards

Cook is intent upon innovating in education and being the first to try something is an additional incentive for him. The Roger Award, recognition for a staff member who has exceeded expectations, is a way to reward those staff members who have demonstrated their understanding of the culture that Cook wants to cultivate. At the staff gathering before the Christmas holidays he calls the name of every nominee for the award. They come out of the audience amid cheers from their colleagues. They receive a token of recognition as a nominee and sit in a group facing the rest of the staff.

Then with much fanfare, one by one the names of the nine Roger Award recipients are called. They come up, are greeted again by Cook and are handed a medal and a check for $500. This is the TCS version of the Academy Awards. These nine or ten staff members are singled out as exemplars of performance-based education. They are the rock stars of this education community.

Teacher Recognition

The staff celebration before the Christmas break resembles a homecoming pep rally. Of course, there is the food and desserts, but the energy level is extreme. For the football coach in Roger Cook, this is a chance to recount the victories of the first half of the season and pump his team up for the hard work that remains in second half of the season. It is an opportunity to thank his staff for all of their hard work during the first four months, but to do so loudly and with a great deal of flourish. There are banners and lights and decorations and videos.

As the staff takes their seat in the Taylor County High School gym, they each find a 200 dollar check taped underneath.

Student Recognition

At the end of the school year, TCS students are packed into the high school gym. Tori Gatewood and Maddie Gumm have been busy all year lining up prizes from the local community. For a small district the array is remarkable, with a retail value of over 10,000 dollars. Every student is given chances to win prizes based upon their test results. If they have gotten the highest category (distinguished), they get five tickets in the raffle. If they score the second highest category (proficient), they are given four tickets for the raffle. This too is a celebration of effort, but the game of chance makes it less of an if-then reward and more happenstance.

The biggest prize of the day is given to one of the graduating seniors. For the past three years Cook has worked with a local car dealer to find a serviceable car to give to a deserving senior. In the past he has found cars that were confiscated as part of an arrest and purchased them at a reduced price. They would be restored and put into good mechanical condition by the school district mechanics. The car is then given as a reward to a high school graduate, whose ticket is pulled from the box. As you can imagine, this is a big deal. There are stories among the staff about sixth graders saying they are going to continue to do their best because they want to win the car when they graduate.

Sharing the spotlight

While Roger Cook has received his share of national awards and recognition, he is quick to turn the spotlight on his staff. At his presentations at the National School Boards Association conference, his board members and senior staff are on the podium. When he receives a national award for the progress he has made with instructional technology, he is quick to praise his staff, saying he could not accomplish this without their help.

At a recent panel discussion at Stanford University on personalized education, he told the group of faculty that board support and the help of his staff made the changes that he has engineered possible.

Sometimes this leads to surprises. At a recent presentation in Nashville, Board of Education Chairman Tony Davis, admitted that when the board agreed to hire Roger Cook, they didn't know what they were getting. "I knew he had a reputation for being good with budgets, but I had no idea that he would be able to do so much for the students of Taylor County."

Visitor tours are scheduled once a month in Taylor County. These tours are a minimally disruptive way to introduce other districts and other educators to performance-based education. During the tours, laced with humorous stories from Cook, he will recognize the accomplishments of the faculty and students he takes visitors to see. He praises the students and staff that have received private pilot licenses as a result of their work in the aviation section. He may ask the students in the student-run bank if he can get a loan for lunch today or praise Patricia Rodgers for her role in facilitating this enterprise.

During one tour he runs into Kelly Milburn in the hallway at the high school and says her work with the S.T.A.R.S. program is outstanding. He introduces Brian Cook (no relation) whom he credits with making the technology programs a success.

NOTES

1. Dwyer, Carol. *Using Praise to Enhance Student Resilience and Learning*. Washington: American Pschological Association, 2015.

2. Dwyer, Carol. *Using Praise to Enhance Student Resilience and Learning*. Ibid.

3. Gunderson, E. A., S. J. Romero, C. Gripshover, C. S. Goldin-Meadow, S. Dweck, and S. C. Levine. "Parent praise to 1–3 year olds predicts children's motivational frameworks 5 years later." *Child Development*, 2013: 1526–541.

4. Henderlong, Jennifer, and Mark Lepper. "The Effects of Praise on Children's Intrinsic Motivation: A Review and Synthesis." *Pschological Bulletin*, 2002: 774–95.

5. Izuma, Keise, Daisuke N. Saito, and Norihiro Sadato. "Processing of social and monetary rewards in the human striatum." *Neuron*, 2008: 284–94.

6. Pink, Daniel H. *Drive*. New York: Riverhead Books, 2009.

7. Kohn, Alfie. *Punished by Rewards: The Trouble with Gold Stars, Incentive Plans, A's, Praise, and Other Bribes*. Boston: Houghton Mifflin, 1993.

8. Pink, Daniel H. *Drive*. New York: Riverhead Books, 2009. Ibid.

9. Brown, Dr. Brené. *Daring Greatly: How the Courage to Be Vulnerable Transforms the Way We Live, Love, Parent, and Lead.* New York: Gotham Books, 2012.
10. Brown, Dr. Brené. *Daring Greatly: How the Courage to Be Vulnerable Transforms the Way We Live, Love, Parent, and Lead.* Ibid.

FOURTEEN
Collaboration

> *A great irony is emerging from the prolonged "education wars" between teacher's unions and supporters of market-based reforms that rely heavily on motivating school personnel by threatening them. The low-income districts and schools that have demonstrated the greatest improvement in student outcomes are generally characterized by deep collaboration between administrators and teachers.* —Greg Anrig[1]

THEORY

The theory of "loose-coupling," an isolation of the instructional core from administrative functions,[2] explains why collaboration when it does occur among the teaching staff often occurs at the administrative level and not at the technical core of education. Yet, as the quote above illustrates, deep collaboration (i.e. on classroom methodology) appears to be the source of the greatest improvement in student outcomes.

"In trying to improve American public schools, educators, policymakers, and philanthropists are overselling the role of the highly skilled, individual teacher and undervaluing the benefits that come from teacher collaborations that strengthen skills, competence, and a school's overall social capital."[3]

Time

One of the reasons that collaboration within the teaching corps is a scarce commodity is the lack of time. And the lack of time seems to be a particularly American issue.

The Organization for Economic Cooperation and Development has created a testing protocol for member states' for fifteen-year-olds every three years. The Programme for International Student Assessment (PISA) according to many is an exam that has not demonstrated the effectiveness of American education on the world stage. American students are barely above the average in reading and far below average in math.

Along with test results PISA also records data on class size and teacher workload. And while the results on class size are inconclusive, the results on teacher workload are not.

"Every single country that outperforms us has significantly smaller teacher workloads. Indeed, on the scale of time devoted by teachers to in-class instruction annually, the United States is off the charts. We spend far more hours in the classroom on average, twice and nearly three times more in some cases, than teachers in any other OECD country save Chile." Compared to 1,051 hours in the United States, Finland clocks 553 and Japan 500.[4]

Elements of Reform

Carrie Leana, an organizational researcher from The University of Pittsburgh, summarizes the tenants of current educational reform this way: "These three beliefs—in the power of teacher human capital, the value of outsiders, and the centrality of the principal in instructional practice—form the implicit or explicit core of many reform efforts today."

And while all three of these elements clearly contribute to better outcomes, the role of social capital, and not human capital, is undervalued, according to Leana. Her analysis and the results of her research challenge the idea that the individual teacher and principal are the source of leadership in effective public education. Instead, social capital—the relationships among teachers—is central to improving the quality of public schools. She says improvement in public education is a result of teachers working together, rather than high performing educators working individually.[5]

Social Capital

From her research, Leana has reached three conclusions.

First, she suggests that the current focus on credentialing will not significantly improve outcomes. Instead we must invest in measures that enhance deep collaboration and sharing of information around teaching and learning, such as mentoring novice teachers.

Second, she has found direct positive relationships between gains in outcomes in mathematics, teacher tenure at grade level, and social capital, and believes the current political efforts to undercut teacher stability and experience may come at a very serious cost.

Third, her results did not see a correlation between principals spending time especially on instructional issues and student achievement, rather those principals who spent more of their time building relationships by collaborating with people and organizations saw gains in outcomes.

All three of these elements of social capital relate to building a culture of collaboration. "(W)hen the relationships among teachers in a school are characterized by high trust and frequent interaction—that is, when social capital is strong—student achievement scores improve."[6]

How do Schools Learn?

In an article in *Educational Administration* entitled, "Creating Smarter Schools through Collaboration," Meagan Tschannen-Moran and her colleagues point out that since our views of student cognition have changed to recognize the value of social constructs and specific contexts, so too our views of how schools themselves learn should change as well.

They point out that organizational knowledge is embedded in the school's beliefs and mirrored in its organizational structure, teaching practices, discipline, curriculum, stories, and celebrations. Organizational knowledge is distributed and social.

"Organizations that appropriately tap the knowledge of various members in decision making become smarter. These shared decision making processes also expand the system's capacity for innovation and invention. But to capitalize on social process in decision making requires the cultivation of a culture of mutual respect, individual and joint responsibility, and a level of discourse in which ideas are freely shared and explored."[7]

Professional Learning Communities

Professional learning communities or communities of practice can be school-based, district-based, cross-disciplinary or content-oriented, statewide, regional, national or international. They are comprised of a group of educators and sometimes stakeholders who are working together to analyze and improve their professional practice. This work is often informed by the use of data, instructionally oriented, and focused on results.

One common characteristic of all effective professional learning communities is collaboration. "These professional learning communities provide opportunities for adults across a school system to learn and think together about how to improve their practice in ways that lead to improved student achievement. This kind of collaboration is rarely found in more traditional types of professional development or in common staff meeting time."[8]

Research on Collaborative Teachers

In 2009 The Teacher's Network studied a group of 1,210 teachers to try and understand the role that collaboration with colleagues plays in teacher efficacy, effectiveness, and stability of assignment. Their data leads to the conclusion that collaboration between and among teachers gives them a vehicle by which effective teaching practices are spread into a school's culture, thereby improving outcomes, and increasing the retention of the most accomplished teachers in high-needs schools."[9]

Over 90 percent of the teachers that were surveyed reported that the collaboration with other professionals in their network had improved their teaching. And 75 percent of those surveyed felt that the collaboration had improved their school.

Research done by the Center for Teaching Quality indicates that educators at every level of expertise benefit from a collaborative professional environment and improve as a result. In fact, the results of the Center's survey strongly suggest that collaboration and networking among teachers is essential to developing teaching talent among existing staff within schools and can make the best teachers even better.[10]

Culture

Sharon Kruse suggests there are five ways in which a collaborative culture can be created or enhanced within a school.

- Specify a quantifiable outcome as a goal. Avoid terms like "success" or "better" since they are not specific. Clearly indicate the purpose of the collaborative effort.
- Diversify and distribute leadership. This allows more work to be accomplished, expands the school's capacity, and builds a strong cohort for future projects.
- Create opportunities for meaningful work. Work with a purpose is easier to accomplish and more rewarding. Organize around shared interests and develop a charge that will focus their collective interest.
- Coordinate efforts with a specific focus on cross-group work. A grade level group might decide to coordinate vertical alignment across grade levels into their work. A group organized around content might decide to combine their work with another group focusing on related content. The issue here is to coordinate the efforts so that individuals don't feel they are working at cross purposes.
- Celebrate collaborative successes. Focus on the individuals that took on new roles and responsibilities in order to complete the project successfully.

"When staff, teachers and parents work together, schools can be happier, healthier places where shared goals are reached and everyone feels a sense of belonging."[11]

PRACTICE

Roger Cook could not make his vision a reality without creating a culture of collaboration that supports that vision. That culture is present in many forms in Taylor County Schools.

When Cook was hired, some teachers were not prepared for his brand of leadership. He tries to visit every classroom on a weekly basis. During the first weeks of his tenure, one teacher called Tony Davis, the chairman of the Board of Education, and asked if there was something wrong with her teaching. When he asked why she was concerned, she told him that the superintendent had come into her classroom.

> "Well did he say anything while he was there?"
> "No," she said. "He just stayed a few minutes and then walked out."
> "I think everything is fine," Davis said. "If there was something wrong, I know Mr. Cook would not have hesitated to tell you."
> Another teacher was so surprised that the superintendent would come into her classroom unannounced, that she promptly fainted. "I think even that teacher is used to me coming in to visit now," Cook says.

Balance

There is a balance that must be achieved in a collaborative environment. Although staff and students alike greet Roger Cook respectfully as he tours the schools, he nonetheless teases some—telling one teacher that he is going to take her classes' iPads away and telling another that he will have to turn the lights out in her classroom because they are out of money.

He is quick to praise both teaches and students for their accomplishments during his tours, noting the kindergarten teacher who started the lost-and-found project with her students will get points toward an award and acknowledging the award-winning aviation students for their success in a statewide competition.

There is also a collegial balance among his district staff. They are all business while solving the next issue that comes through the door, but just as quick to tell one of the many stories about the superintendent's adventures.

Charles Higdon, the assistant superintendent, at dinner after a presentation with the board and the staff at the National School Boards Association annual conference, told the story of Stephan Turnipseed, Executive Director of Strategic Partnerships at LEGO Education, who came to visit

TCS. It was lunch time and Cook realized belatedly he had the responsibility for getting a speaker for the local Rotary luncheon. He asked Turnipseed if he could buy him lunch at the Rotary. On the way to the luncheon, Cook asked if he would mind saying a few words.

The LEGO executive agreed and spoke eloquently for twenty minutes to the group at the luncheon. It wasn't until he left that the staff informed the superintendent that Turnipseed usually got 10,000 dollars for his speaking engagements. The following week Cook told his fellow Rotarians that he was very pleased to have gotten a 10,000 dollar speaker for the price of a lunch.

Frequent Interaction

Although most Taylor County teachers teach with their classroom doors closed, there are numerous interactions that occur on a daily and weekly basis. Laura Benningfield, the principal at Taylor County High School has found that the weekly meetings of the professional learning communities have united her staff to accomplish a common goal. "Sure, personalities are different, but meeting regularly about student success has really brought them closer together." Benningfield is building social capital by promoting a structure that engages the teaching staff collectively in school reform and confirming Carrie Leana's research that building social capital by engaging the teaching staff in collective behavior paves the way to better outcomes.

Benningfield tries to briefly visit each meeting of the professional learning communities about once every two weeks to stay in touch and connect with her staff. She keeps her high school staff informed about issues through a weekly update and e-mails regularly with information she thinks they should know. She uses very little of the early release Friday time for "housekeeping," since that is protected time for professional development.

Tony Jewell sees his school staff as a family and treats them accordingly. "We celebrate our successes and mourn our losses as any family does." Each member of the staff is treated with courtesy and respect and with the knowledge that each and every one has unique gifts that they contribute to the mission of making students successful.

With over 1,200 students and nearly 130 staff, the work of Donna Williams, the principal at Taylor County Elementary, is similar to that of a town manager within the halls of her aging building. (A new elementary school is currently under construction.) There is no doubt that she is aware of everything that is happening in her school, introducing herself to the various tours coming through and answering questions from the guests, but she just as quickly excuses herself and disappears to tend to another issue. Like the other principals her management style is distributed leadership, not micromanagement.

As Charles Higdon explains, "Everyone is expected to do your position well." The climate of each school and of the district staff is one of cooperation and collaboration to accomplish success for each and every student. The latest climate survey at TCS showed 95 percent of the staff love what they are doing.

Nay-Sayers

But everything cannot be perfect. It rains some days even in paradise. Charles Higdon was asked how the leadership deals with a staff member who is uncooperative or not collaborating with their colleagues. There was no hesitation. "It is dealt with immediately."

There is only one thing that frustrates Roger Cook. There are frequent tours through Taylor County Schools as their national reputation grows. Cook personally guides most of them. Conversion to performance-based methodology is hard work, and he doesn't sugar-coat the facts. When visitors' comments become cynical or negative, he sometimes loses patience. "I don't deal well with negativity. If they are not willing to change, I'm not sure why they've come."

Creating Culture

In November 2007 *Harvard Business Review* (HBR) published an article about the eight ways to build collaborative teams. A comparison of the recommended steps to the TCS practice is enlightening, since they are very similar.[12]

The first step recommended is to invest heavily in signature relationship practices (the article cites facility investments as an example). Roger Cook heavily invests his personal time in collaborative activities, like visiting every classroom every week. He also invests heavily in educator collaboration by protecting early release Fridays as professional development. And although district financial resources are limited, he has found a way to begin construction to replace two of three schools in the district.

The second recommendation in the *HBR* article is to set a personal example with executive staff. Roger Cook is not a micromanager. He sets an example of collaboration with district staff through a distributed leadership model. "Everybody has a job to do, and if we all do it well, we all win."

The third step is to create a "gift culture" by mentoring and coaching on an informal basis and helping people build the networks they need to work across departmental boundaries. This work is celebrated at TCS, both in terms of tangible rewards and in terms of personal recognition. Cook not only supports peer-to-peer tutoring by educators, but through his S.T.A.R.S. program, he supports and encourages students to mentor other students. "Everybody's not good at everything. Sometimes you need help."

Ensuring the requisite skills is the fourth step. There is a focus within TCS on the acquisition of the "soft skills" within TCS for students and staff—communication, building relationships, and resolving issues innovatively. Cook praises the ingenuity of his maintenance staff for figuring out a way to repair the chiller at the high school. The price from the local Trane dealer was almost 100,000 dollars. The maintenance department repaired the equipment for ten-thousand dollars. And Cook immediately connects it to the instructional mission. "You know how many iPads I can buy for ninety-thousand dollars?"

Step five is supporting a strong sense of community. TCS does this through a variety of vehicles. There are academic pep rallies and teacher appreciation days. There are turkeys given to the staff on Thanksgiving, and Roger Awards given to teachers for extraordinary work. The community at large is also included with outreach from student internships to support of those adults in the community who are in need of a high school diploma.

Assigning team leaders that are both task- and relationship-oriented is the next step. Cook selects his TCS leadership team with these qualifications in mind. They get things done by working with their colleagues.

The next step is building heritage relationships. Roger Cook wants all of his students to think about becoming teachers. To date fifty-three of the TCS certified staff are alumni. The teacher corps is remarkably stable. The quote heard most often from the staff is "I cannot imagine working anywhere else!"

Understanding role clarity and task ambiguity is the last *Harvard Business Review* recommendation.[13] While everyone at Taylor County has position clarity, stories of collaboration and crossover are plentiful. This is not an organization that rigidly defines task responsibilities. "We are all here to help one another," says Cook.

This review of the steps in the article is certainly not meant to imply that Roger Cook read the article and sought to follow those recommendations. On the contrary, as a veteran educator and coach, he knew what needed to happen in order to create a culture of collaboration and set about to accomplish it. What is remarkable is that he was able to do it intuitively.

When Roger Cook presents either at a conference or to visitors on a tour, he quickly points out that he is a practitioner and a problem-solver, not a theorist. He knows what will work because he has tried it or analyzed a similar practice. Unlike those that analyze data points and suggest methodology as a result, he identifies a problem, proposes a solution, discusses it with seasoned practitioners and creates a pragmatic solution. "Sometimes what we try doesn't work. And that's okay, because it teaches us about what will work."

However, when asked if he ever did something that didn't work, Cook was stumped. He e-mailed his staff and asked if they could remember anything that they had tried that didn't ultimately work, and they could not think of anything. The measure of whether or not something fails is not if it works the first time it is tried, but whether or not you are willing to continue to modify it until it works the way you want. TCS continues to tinker with a methodology until it performs the way they want it to perform. And then they continue to try and improve it.

NOTES

1. Strauss, Valerie. "Why collaboration is vital to creating effective schools." *Washington Post*, May 2, 2013.
2. Elmore, Richard F. *School Reform from the Inside Out*. Cambridge: Harvard University Press, 2004.
3. Leana, Carrie R. "The Missing Link in School Reform." *The Stanford Social Innovation Review*, 2011.
4. Mosle, Sara. "Building Better Teachers." *The Atlantic*, September 2014.
5. Leana, Carrie R. "The Missing Link in School Reform." *Ibid.*
6. Leana, Carrie R. "The Missing Link in School Reform." *Ibid.*
7. Tschannen-Moran, Megan, Cynthia Uline, Anita Woolfork Hoy, and Timm Mackley. "Creating Smarter Schools Through Collaboration." *Journal of Educational Administration*, 2000: 247–71.
8. Tschannen-Moran, Megan, Cynthia Uline, Anita Woolfork Hoy, and Timm Mackley. "Creating Smarter Schools Through Collaboration." *Ibid.*
9. *Professional Development Strategies that Improve School Reform*. Providence, RI: Annenburg Institute for School Reform, 2004.
10. Berry, Barnett, Alesha Daughtry, and Alan Wieder. *Collaboration: Closing the Effective Teaching Gap*. Carrboro, NC: Center for Teaching Quality, 2009.
11. Kruse, Sharon. "5 Ways to Build a Culture of Collaboration with Staff, Teachers and Parents." American Association of School Administrators. March 2010. http://wwwold.aasa.org/content.aspx?id=12512 (accessed April 26, 2015).
12. Gratton, Lynda, and Tamara J. Erickson. "Eight Ways to Build Collaborative Teams." Harvard Business Review, 2007.
13. Gratton, Lynda, and Tamara J. Erickson. "Eight Ways to Build Collaborative Teams." *Ibid.*

The Beginning

"It always seems impossible until it's done." —*Nelson Mandela*

What can be learned from this overview of a high successful small public school district in the middle of Kentucky? What makes their ideas special or unique? Can the elements and methodologies be taken to scale or are they a one-off solution to a local condition?

What Taylor County Schools has accomplished is reproducible and can be adapted to local conditions. Every school district in the United States struggles to keep some students in school. What Roger Cook has done is develop a program that keeps every student connected to the district. From his first day in Taylor County he has adapted schedules, program delivery, and pedagogy to each child's needs and aggressively identified those who would otherwise drop out and provided them with alternatives.

Luckily, the fourteen methods described are flexible tools, not part of a hard and fast structure that must be rigidly followed. While not every one can be incorporated into every school district, these ideas are a place to begin both a conversation and a new paradigm.

It is important to remember, however, that structures and tools are only as good as the attitude of the education team that sets out to implement them. Fidelity of implementation is strictly dependent upon the vision and mission as expressed by district leadership and how the teachers and administrators interpret that vision.

Leading

Roger Cook believes that you must lead from the front—setting a clear and consistent vision for the district is the superintendent's job. He also believes that it is a standard that is measured each and every day at Taylor County Schools. Every teacher and every administrator in Taylor County knows that no child should be held back, no child will fail, and no child will drop out.

But to Cook leading from the front does not mean telling people what to do, it means telling them what you want to accomplish, and helping them to develop the skills to make that happen and using others' ideas as well as your own. One reason that Cook is so successful with his programs is that he vets them with everyone before he begins, and during that vetting process he changes the program in response to the comments he gets.

The self-paced online lessons are just one example of how this works. After seeing a program on Khan Academy, he asked his staff to create a similar program. While they started by using Khan Academy lessons, the staff soon found that lessons prepared by TCS teachers connected better with students. They also found that a traditional flipped classroom did not give them the results they wanted, so they created self-paced learning. What began strictly as a duplication, soon morphed into an entirely different educational format.

By asking teachers to volunteer to design this format, Cook got enthusiastic engagement and not just compliance. His volunteers became experts and are now working at the state and regional levels to assist other school districts as well as Taylor County in supplementing curriculum with technology tools. This is also typical of his leadership style. Expertise developed within Taylor County Schools has led to staff being offered promotions in other districts.

Positive results from the school climate surveys do not come without leadership effort. There is tremendous support for the work of the teachers and administrators at TCS. This is not just lip service, but a genuine appreciation for the teaching and learning, including rewards and encouragement. There is an understanding that changing the paradigm in the classroom is the only way to effect authentic educational reform and produce the successful graduates that all school systems want and that paradigm shift is only accomplished through the communal hard work of the education professionals in the schools.

Change of this magnitude is not easy regardless of what phase of leadership your district is in. There are multiple issues to be considered, both practical and political. These are some of the most obvious:

Purpose

Clarity of purpose is necessary for a successful change in methodology to performance-based education. A statement of purpose should be simple, concise, and free of extraneous content or terminology that may be used to define a particular political position. It is important that this is something upon which everyone can agree.

Scope

The scope of a major change must be districtwide. If it is presented as a parallel methodology to traditional pedagogy, it will never be taken to scale. The staff must understand that regardless of how it is introduced, whether it is one school, a group of schools, or an entire feeder system, that the intention is to convert the entire district to this methodology.

Communication

Many districts think of communication as mono-directional, the need to push messages out to the community on a regular basis. While that is certainly important for transparency, listening for stakeholder input is just as important.

Support

An effort to change is not a solo performance. Without the support of your board, it is doomed to failure. Without the enthusiastic support of the influencers on your staff, it will not work. Performance-based education is a novel way of looking at pedagogy. Similar to those dual visual images posted on social media. If you want to make performance-based education a reality in your district, you must spend enough time in explanation that everyone can see the second image rather than the initial one. Cook likes to describe the change as the "end of education as we know it."

This type of change must also have parent and taxpayer support as well. Roger Cook's approach to the community is simple, but also very subtle. What parent is going to resist an effort to place their child in the educational environment in which they learn best?

Consistency

Senior educators that have been subjected to an untold number of new ideas are looking for consistency. Frequent correlation between what is said and what is done is the only way to convince those who are skeptical that the proposed changes are authentic.

Strategy and Reach

A well-conceived strategy will include a hierarchy in which each educator is proximate to leadership that believes in the vision. Of course, this is far more difficult in a large district than in a small one. Leadership at the regional and area levels must be converts to performance-based education. Cook's span of influence is roughly 400 staff members. When he was asked how broadly that could be expanded, he felt he would be comfortable with double that number.

Clearly, distributed leadership is critical for taking performance-based education to scale. Administrators at the regional or area levels must be given the authority to make decisions that correspond to the vision. Targeted delegation must occur.

Continuous assessment and analysis

Monitor progress continuously. Draw conclusions from those results. Act upon those conclusions. And communicate the results.

Staffing

Hire for attitude and train accordingly. Very few staff members, if any, will know about implementing performance-based education. Willingness to learn something new is an essential qualification.

Logistics

Building an organization that innovates on a daily basis takes fortitude and persistence. It is neither easy, nor quick. The experience of Taylor County Schools has demonstrated that it is rewarding. A target schedule for completion of the change should be publicized. Tomorrow is too soon. Five years from now is too far away.

Mistakes

Roger Cook and his team have made a few mistakes. But when asked to identify what didn't work, they have a hard time naming anything. Not because they are not honest, but because rather than discarding a trial methodology as not productive, they tinker with it and discuss it until they get it to work, and then they tinker some more to make it even better.

More than sixty school districts from all over the United States have toured Taylor County Schools during the past several years. The district and their superintendent have won numerous national and statewide awards. They have presented their methodology at multiple conferences.

But nothing is easy in the age of legislated accountability and mandated high stakes testing. The degree of difficulty to transition from a traditional program to performance-based education is high. However, this should not dissuade you from moving toward a program that works. Nothing is more important than ensuring the success of each and every student. After all, the cost of continuing to do nothing at all is far greater than the cost of doing something.

About the Author

Mike Raible has worked in education for more than two decades, serving as a member of the executive staff for two school districts and as CEO of his own firm, The School Solutions Group. In his practice Raible connects verbal, visual, and audio imagery to help clients be specific about their goals and improve key processes to reach those goals. He lives with his family in Charlotte, North Carolina.

www.ingramcontent.com/pod-product-compliance
Lightning Source LLC
Chambersburg PA
CBHW030142240426
43672CB00005B/230